VANCOUVER **TRAIL RUNNING**

THE GOOD, THE RAD & THE GNARLY

QUICKDRAW
PUBLICATIONS

BY RICH WHEATER

QUICKDRAW
PUBLICATIONS

POSTAL ADDRESS
PO Box 5313
Squamish, BC V8B 0C2, Canada

CONTACT US
(604) 892-9271
info@quickdrawpublications.com
www.quickdrawpublications.com

Quickdraw Publications is constantly expanding our range of guidebooks. If you have a manuscript or an idea for a book, please get in touch.

Designed and typeset in Canada; printed and bound in China.

FIRST EDITION, 2ND PRINTING

INTERNATIONAL STANDARD BOOK NUMBER
ISBN 978-0-9732593-8-4

AUTHOR
Rich Wheater
info@richwheater.com
www.richwheater.com

PHOTOGRAPHY
All photographs by the author unless otherwise noted. Cover: Senja Palonen running across Hollyburn Mountain on the *Baden-Powell Trail*. Page one: Kristina Jenei on the *Baden-Powell Trail* at the base of Mount Fromme. This page: Senja Palonen cruising through a lush, coastal forest.

Give Us Your Feedback

To help improve everyone's trail running experience in Vancouver, we need your feedback! After using this book, please help us by providing information about your experiences. We welcome suggestions and corrections. Contact us at info@quickdrawpublications.com or info@richwheater.com.

Disclaimer

Read this before you use this book!

Trail running, walking and hiking are potentially dangerous activities involving inherent risks that could result in serious injury or death. This book serves only as a compilation of information and the author is not responsible for any inaccuracies. This guidebook does not serve as a substitute for adequate experience, judgment, route planning, physical conditioning, equipment selection, or appropriate route selection. Changes in roadways, trails, weather, trail conditions, signage, waterways and seasons are to be expected, and discrepancies are not the responsibility of the author or Quickdraw Publications. The author, publisher and distributors of this book assume no responsibility for the welfare of the user.

Epic North Shore backcounty *The northward view from the summit of Mt. Seymour*

ACKNOWLEDGEMENTS

For starters, I'd like to thank everyone who believed in and supported this project. Many people leant their enthusiasm, suggestions, constructive criticism and companionship during the creation of this book. You know who you are and you all deserve a keg party!

I'd also like to acknowledge race organizers, retailers, running clubs and volunteers who passionately promote trail running through web sites and community events. And thanks to the folks from the Burnaby Mountain Bike Club, North Shore Mountain Bike Association (NSMBA), North Shore Athletics, Mountain Equipment Coop (MEC), parks employees and all others who continually assist with trail maintenance.

A huge nod goes to Marc Bourdon at Quickdraw Publications who offered continual guidance (read: monastic patience) throughout this endeavor. His talents as a graphic designer and meticulous publisher have helped this project blossom from a fistful of boring Word documents into an attractive guidebook. Secretly, I always wanted this book to occupy a spot on the coffee table or in the bathroom's toilet-side magazine tote. With Marc's help I think we've made that possible!

And finally, I'm especially lucky to have the endless, unconditional support of Senja Palonen and my tireless pooch Daisy, my life partners and most frequent trail companions.

*This book is dedicated to
the Mud, the Blood
& the Beer.*

Welcome to Vancouver *Evening light on downtown, as seen from Spanish Banks near Pacific Spirit Park.*

INTRODUCTION

Welcome to Vancouver, one of the most exciting and exotic trail running destinations in the world! Here in the temperate rainforest, you'll find trails of all kinds: beachfront cruises, gently flowing singletrack, technical minefields and desperate hill climbs. Indeed, the legendary North Shore mountains serve as an epic backdrop for this vibrant west coast city, where a plethora of trails provide a lifetime of exploration for mud-hungry endurance fiends. Lace your shoes tight and prepare to get dirty!

ORIENTATION

Getting to Vancouver

Vancouver is located on the south coast of beautiful British Columbia, right on the 49th parallel. From the east, the city can be accessed by Trans-Canada Highway 1, or from the south via Highway 99 (Interstate 5 if you are heading north from the United States). Downtown is about one hour north of the Canada–U.S. border. Alternatively, you can fly into the beautiful Vancouver International Airport (YVR). Trains, coaches and cruise lines also offer services to Vancouver.

Around Town

Vancouver is a major cosmopolitan center where one can indulge in all aspects of urban living: art gallery tours, a killer live music scene, pubs and nightclubs, trade shows, world-class shopping, major-league sports and thousands of awesome restaurants representing cuisine from every corner of the globe. Add to this Vancouver's unique coastal situation at the foot of the rugged North Shore Mountains and you have plenty of opportunity for outdoor recreation within minutes of a five-star urban venue.

Three commercial ski resorts cap the North Shore Mountains: Cypress Bowl (2010 Olympic Games venue), Grouse Mountain and Mount Seymour. Grouse offers the only gondola service from base to alpine and feels like an alpine Disneyland with helicopter tours, zip lines, a live lumberjack show and resident grizzly bears! All three mountains give incredible views of the city and surrounding waterways, and provide convenient access to rugged backcountry.

About the Trails

Vancouver trails vary dramatically; the area has everything from wide, flat gravel paths to remote alpine gnarr. Most of the runs in this book travel through a rainforest brimming with second-growth cedar, Douglas fir and western hemlock trees. Giant sword ferns blanket the ground and countless streams and creeks carve intricate grooves down steep hillsides. The trail surfaces tend to be quite loamy and covered in soft forest debris. While there is a healthy selection of novice trails, the defining character of this area is one of extraordinarily technical trails packed with loose rocks, man-eating mud-pits and twisted roots that will challenge your cadence and agility.

About This Book

Vancouver's countless hiking trails are well documented, but not all are suitable for running. Many are too steep or difficult and others are just plain boring or unaesthetic. This book weeds out the riff-raff and showcases over 40 superb circuits sure to challenge your inner mountain goat and whip you into shape! Throughout the book you'll find numerous colour-coded maps packed with accurate trail renderings and detailed route descriptions ranging from easy half-

hour urban leg-stretchers to four-hour mountain epics.

In addition, I've provided information pertaining to mountain travel, equipment, technique, cross-training and personal safety. I highly recommend all runners read this stuff, regardless of experience or ability. The local mountains are exceptionally rugged and will punish those who underestimate the conditions and terrain. Armed with this guidebook you'll be well prepared for many safe, enjoyable adventures.

What Areas Does This Book Cover?

Geographically, this book documents trail runs from Horseshoe Bay to Deep Cove (the North Shore), as well as circuits in Vancouver proper, which include the magnificent Pacific Spirit Park and Stanley Park. In addition, I've included the following park areas east of Vancouver: Burnaby Mountain Conservation Reserve, Burnaby Lake and Port Moody, the latter of which features Buntzen Lake and Belcarra Regional Park. I've also detailed a few paved pathways that are regional classics and popular with runners. To orient yourself to these trail running areas, please review the overview map on the following page.

You may find some of these circuits difficult to run "on- sight", meaning that trail junctions may not be marked and some are outright vague. Pay attention to the descriptions to avoid "accidental exploration". It may take several attempts at following some circuits before you feel the flow. Once you're familiar with these trails you'll want to spice things up. Try doing a familiar run in reverse. Add or subtract distance, or start from a different trailhead. Truth is, you'll experience more freedom and adventure once you put this book down and begin exploring on your own.

Origins

When you think about it, it's obvious that cavemen were the first trail runners. They ran to migrate, keep warm and escape threatening tribes or animals. They were hard-core! They didn't have specialized footwear, wicking fabrics, energy gels or water bladders, and they certainly didn't run for enjoyment or fitness. Want proof? Watch *Quest For Fire*, it's awesome!

Through time, humans began to run for fun, fitness and competition. Efforts to break records on established courses (such as the marathon or mile) became a natural part of the sport's progression. For years we've recognized numerous sub-categories such as relays, triathlons and track & field. Nowadays it seems everyone's getting "back to nature" and enjoying the great outdoors, so it's no surprise that trail running has emerged as sub-sport all its own.

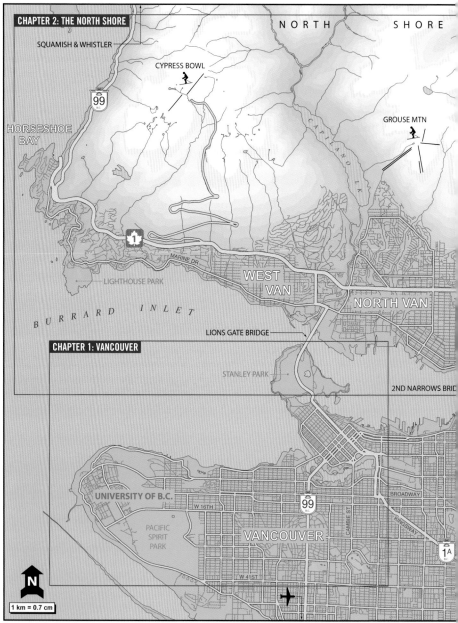

SQUAMISH & WHISTLER

CYPRESS BOWL

NORTH   SHORE

99
B.C.

HORSESHOE
BAY

GROUSE MTN

CAPILANO LK

1

MARINE DR

WEST
VAN

NORTH VAN

LIGHTHOUSE PARK

BURRARD   INLET

LIONS GATE BRIDGE

CHAPTER 1: VANCOUVER

STANLEY PARK

2ND NARROWS BRID

UNIVERSITY OF B.C.

W 16TH

BROADWAY

99
B.C.

CAMBIE ST

KINGSWAY

PACIFIC
SPIRIT
PARK

VANCOUVER

1A
B.C.

W 41ST

N

1 km = 0.7 cm

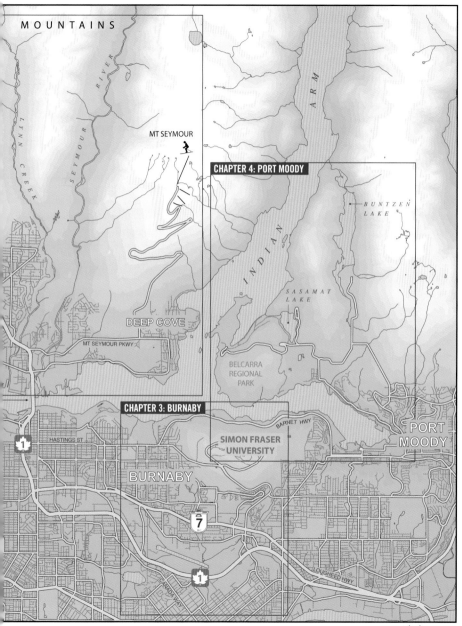

MOUNTAINS

SEYMOUR RIVER

LYNN CREEK

SEYMOUR

MT SEYMOUR

CHAPTER 4: PORT MOODY

ARM

INDIAN

BUNTZEN LAKE

SASAMAT LAKE

DEEP COVE

MT SEYMOUR PKWY

BELCARRA REGIONAL PARK

CHAPTER 3: BURNABY

BARNET HWY

SIMON FRASER UNIVERSITY

PORT MOODY

HASTINGS ST

BURNABY

7

CANADA WAY

LOUGHEED HWY

CODE OF CONDUCT

Trail running is a wonderfully simple, unobtrusive activity. When running, you're not likely to annoy anyone or damage the environment. However, there are a few issues worth mentioning with regards to environmental etiquette and personal conduct.

Trail Etiquette

On multi-use trails, be courteous and friendly to other trail users. Warn of your approach and pass on the left. The code for these trails is this: hikers yield to equestrians (horses) and mountain bikers yield to all other users. If unsure, be courteous and yield.

Specially built mountain bike trails require more consideration. Mountain biking is extremely popular in Vancouver and the cycling community has worked very hard to construct and maintain their beloved trails. Mountain bike trails are difficult to walk on and are often packed with insane architecture. If you choose to run on a specific mountain bike trail, it's essential that *you* yield to riders. Mountain bikes move very quickly and can creep up on you with little warning. Turn off your iPod and keep your head up! You don't want to get nailed by a mountain bike.

Respect

Stay on main trails. Cutting switchbacks hastens erosion and creates unwanted trail braiding. Avoid steep descents in sloppy conditions and be aware that dodging puddles widens trails. Be respectful of wildlife and habitat enhancement projects, and leash your dog when noted and when near wildlife.

Trail Closures

Trails get closed for many reasons: washouts, downed timber, ecosystem rehabilitation, nesting birds, trail maintenance, etc. Respect and abide by all posted closures.

Garbage

Littering sucks. Don't do it! If you stumble across garbage please pack it out. Dirt-bags who litter are obviously lazy and inconsiderate. Most trailheads have garbage and/or recycling containers. Please use them.

Dogs

Dogs are awesome running companions, but not everyone loves them. Be prepared to leash your dog and carry poop bags to pick up after your pup. The general rule in most Metro Vancouver and B.C. parks is dogs must be leashed, although many parks have designated off-leash zones.

You may encounter commercial dog-walkers on the trail, sometimes with nearly ten dogs in hand! Personally, I don't think it's possible to fully control a pack this size and when the posse gets excited, it can be intimidating. If you encounter this scenario, I recommend slowing down a little and passing cautiously so your Olympic momentum doesn't incite a ruckus.

When Nature Calls

Use toilet or outhouse facilities whenever possible. If you must perform in the forest, wander off-trail 100 metres or so, kick a hole and bury your business at least six inches down. Burn your toilet paper or pack it out.

Code of Conduct *Top to bottom: The beast in question; the North Shore's nicest outhouse at Whyte Lake; no dogs allowed at White Pine Beach.*

PERSONAL SAFETY & NAVIGATION

Be prepared! This well-known Scout's Motto is simple and true. Still, every year people get lost or injured in Vancouver's mountains because they are ill equipped for their activity. Always tell someone where you're going and when you expect to return, and consider carrying items on the Be Prepared list.

Back at the car keep a change of clothes, water and a snack for when you've finished. You'll probably be hungry, cold, tired and wet after running. Having this stuff on hand will help you get dry and comfortable after your workout.

Solo Running

Running solo is very relaxing and one of the best ways to clear your mind and mentally reboot. Physically it's safe, but definitely heed the Scout's Motto since there will be no one to help you if you run into trouble. Allow plenty of daylight and avoid running unfamiliar terrain alone.

Be particularly cautious of solo running in areas such as Pacific Spirit (UBC) or Stanley Park, as these locations have a history of suspicious activity. If you run solo in these areas I recommend that you stick to popular trails during busy daylight hours.

Cell Phones

Cell phones can be vital in case of emergency, but don't count on reception, especially in the North Shore mountains. Try to gain a high point with minimal tree cover. Gullies, creek drainages, cliff bands etc. all serve as blockades to cell reception. When running, keep the phone *off* to preserve battery power and protect the unit by sealing it in a waterproof bag such as a Ziploc, or a small, hard-shell case such as those made by Pelican or Otter. If an emergency arises, call 911.

Maps

Always carry a detailed map and description of the trail you plan to run. Try to maintain a consistent orientation and learn to use a topographic map such as those in this book; they are best because they accurately display elevation contours and terrain features such as peaks, saddles, ridges and valleys.

Global Positioning System (GPS)

GPS uses a worldwide network of radio signals and satellites to determine your spot on Earth with remarkable accuracy. A handheld GPS receiver gives your location in either UTM or latitude and longitude coordinates. GPS units are not error-free and can lose reception under thick forest canopies, in deep canyons or around cliffs. They are also battery powered and can fail in cold or excessively wet conditions. As such they shouldn't be relied upon exclusively, but can be an excellent tool when used with a topographic map. These things are finicky; training and practice is a must.

Getting Lost

Most of the runs in this book follow well-traveled and well-mapped trails. Along the way though, you'll pass by many unmarked and/or minor paths. Take time to familiarize yourself with trail networks and primary arteries (such as the *Baden-Powell Trail*). These are exceptionally well defined and usually offer a bailout to popular trailheads and residential areas.

To avoid getting lost, STAY ON THE TRAIL. Pay attention to signage and watch for colored markers on trees, a cairn (small pile of stones) or flagging tape. Keep your head UP and take note of your surroundings as you run. Landmarks such as boardwalks, creeks, bridges, signs, gullies and cliffs all serve to define your location. If you become unsure of the way, it may be best to retrace your steps to a known point or retreat altogether.

If you get lost or benighted, STAY PUT. Seek shelter, put on all your clothes and huddle for warmth. Light a fire if possible. It will not only keep you warm, but smoke will assist a rescue party. Most people who get lost underestimate the terrain and are ill prepared and/or inexperienced. They lack fitness, proper clothing, survival equipment, maps and other navigational tools. Understand that Vancouver has some of the wildest mountain terrain and weather on the planet. Your safety is your responsibility.

Every year rescue parties assist numerous people from wilderness predicaments. If you think you are lost, hunker down and call 911.

Be Prepared

- ☐ Map/GPS/Trail description
- ☐ Basic first-aid kit (pain killers, moleskin for blisters, bee sting kit, etc.)
- ☐ Swiss-army knife
- ☐ Emergency space blanket
- ☐ Cell phone (may NOT get reception)
- ☐ Snack
- ☐ Water
- ☐ Waterproof matches or lighter
- ☐ Shell jacket
- ☐ Gloves
- ☐ Toque
- ☐ Whistle
- ☐ Headlamp
- ☐ Dog

HAZARDS

Variable Trail Conditions

Vancouver routinely gets hammered by foul weather for weeks at a time, making trails much more difficult to run. Winter conditions are typically very wet, slippery and muddy. Every spring park employees and volunteers clear deadfall, rebuild washed-out bridges and reroute trails. Check with Metro Vancouver Parks for specific trail closures or warnings.

Exposure

When planning your run, understand that mountain weather can change very quickly and you should be prepared for extreme weather conditions any time of the year. Pack appropriate clothing, keeping in mind that whatever the ambient temperature is in the city, it will be 10-15 degrees cooler (even more with wind-chill) in the alpine. On the flip side, sun exposure can also be troublesome. Wear sunscreen, a hat and pack water to stay protected from dehydration and harmful UV rays.

Hypothermia

This life-threatening condition usually occurs when it's cold, windy and wet – a common theme in this neck of the woods. If not prepared for such conditions, your body may not be able to maintain it's normal functioning temperature and will gradually shut down.

Hypothermia victims are usually oblivious to what's happening. Watch for uncontrollable shivering, loss of coordination and shallow breathing. A victim may feel nauseous and seem exceptionally fatigued. As things worsen they become dazed and confused. Skin pales, and lips and extremities turn blue. Not good! If this is happening, get the victim out of the elements immediately and remove all wet clothing. Wrap them in warm dry clothes and encourage steady rehydration; hot drinks are great. Help the victim warm-up gradually, as doing so too quickly stresses the heart.

WILDLIFE

British Columbia is famous for an abundance of wildlife and, in the local hills, a variety of critters and beasts may be encountered. Thankfully, only a handful may warrant concern.

Bears

Black bears are common in British Columbia and it's a privilege to see one. However, these fascinating creatures are shy, highly unpredictable and potentially dangerous. Attacks on humans are rare, but bears may be provoked when startled or defending themselves, their young or their food. To avoid an encounter, make noises as you run, such as occasionally hand clapping, chatting or singing. Some people wear bear-bells, but personally I find these totally annoying.

If you see a bear, don't panic. Do not approach or attempt to feed the bear. Talk calmly and slowly back away, avoiding eye contact. Speaking to the bear helps identify you as human and it will probably flee. If the bear approaches, make aggressive, loud noises. Clap your hands, yell and jump around; try to appear big and mean! Most likely, the bear will skedaddle.

Cougars

Cougar sightings are extremely rare, but these massive cats certainly exist. Should you encounter a cougar, stop running immediately and don't take your eyes off it. Make yourself appear as big and aggressive as possible. Grab a huge stick and wave it around. If attacked, fight for your life!

Coyotes

These nocturnal scavengers resemble a fox-like dog and are responsible for the disappearance

Black bear

Cougar

Coyote

FROM TOP: CHRIS GEHLAN, TAMBAKO THE JAGUAR, DON DEBOLD (LAST TWO ON FLICKR.COM)

of many beloved pets. They hunt in packs and often deploy a lure tactic: A lone coyote will lure your dog into the forest, where the rest of the pack awaits. Not just forest creatures, coyotes live throughout the city and have been known to hangout in downtown dumpsters. If you hear a chorus of high-pitch yips and howls, or see a coyote, keep Fido close.

Mosquitoes & Ticks

British Columbia mosquitoes are legendary and most active between May and September. Runners generally move too quickly for them to be a nuisance, but once you stop they'll be all over your salty, sweaty skin. You'll probably be most annoyed when they bombard you during your trailhead stretch. Clothing layers or bug-dope should fend off an attack.

Deer ticks are especially prevalent in the spring and may carry Lyme disease. If these evil little monsters dig into your skin you'll want to extract them pronto. An embedded tick looks like a swollen lentil and they tend to lurk in dark, hairy crevasses. Special pliers can be purchased for removal, but I've found dental floss lassoed around the head works well: Slowly but forcefully pull the tick straight out, twisting slightly, and be sure to extract the head.

Bees & Wasps

A variety of stinging insects exist in Vancouver and are most active in the summer. They typically nest in rotten timber, dead stumps and dry patches of moss. If you disturb a nest, the little devils will be very angry and it's usually the second runner that suffers the wrath. Be sure to carry appropriate medicine if you suspect you're allergic.

Mosquito

Tick

Honey bee

Paper wasp

FROM TOP: GERALD YUVALLO, JERRY KIRKHART, UMBERTO SALVAGNIN, RADU PRIVANTU (ALL ON FLICKR.COM)

EQUIPMENT

One of the great benefits of trail running is the relative minimalism. Yes, there are many accessories that can make running safer and more enjoyable, but overall it's a very equipment-light sport. However, careful consideration should always be given to proper clothing and footwear.

Upper Body Clothing

Proper clothing will not only be more comfortable, but will help keep your core temperature stable and protect you from the elements. For outdoor aerobic activity, I recommend a layering system. A typical layering system includes a base layer for moisture wicking, a mid weight layer for insulation and a shell to block wind or precipitation.

Base layers are made of light, quick-drying synthetic fabrics that are highly breathable and wick moisture away from the skin. Avoid cotton as it retains liquid and takes forever to dry. The mid weight layer should provide modest insulation without being too hot. Try a thin, form-fitted fleece or vest. Finally, if you plan to run in inclement weather or exposed locations, carry a lightweight water-resistant and breathable shell. A windbreaker is usually sufficient for minor drizzles and is light and compressible for stuffing in your pack. If you choose to run in a downpour, understand that a waterproof shell will make you sweat so much you'll get just as wet. In this case, aim to stay warm as opposed to dry. Consider a water-resistant micro-fiber instead of boxy and heavy Gore-Tex.

Lower Body Clothing

For the legs, synthetic shorts are ideal. Short shorts provide more range-of-motion than surf-style trunks, which tend to bind on the legs. In cold conditions, consider tights made of Spandex or Lycra. Tights keep your legs warm without the burden of heavy fabrics. Just don't wear them on the bus – it's not 1985.

For underwear, a synthetic brief works best. A brief holds the family jewels snug and alleviates painful scrotal chafing. Some shorts feature a built-in brief. Never wear boxers, though, or you'll suffer the raw consequences! Women also recommend a brief or low-profile thong and prefer an athletic sports bra for optimal support and moisture wicking.

Footwear

Shoes – Any running shoe will work fine on easy trails, but consider a proper trail shoe if you plan to run on technical ground. Trail running shoes feature widely-spaced, deep lugs for better traction. Softer rubber soles give better grip on slippery surfaces (just like snow tires) and wider outsoles improve stability. Some shoes have a toe bumper for protection against sharp objects, or a shield built into the sole to combat rock bruising. You might want to consider replacing

the liner with a Superfoot brand liner, which gives better support and durability. Some shoes are weather-resistant with a waterproof liner (usually Gore-Tex) and might even come with a low-cut gator to keep out muck and debris. Some models allow studs to be fixed to the outsole for traction on snow or ice, or you can get crampon style attachments such as those made by Yaktrax.

Socks – Always a topic of debate, good running socks are form-fitted and highly breathable. They should be synthetic and offer excellent moisture wicking. I prefer low-cut, thin cycling socks. You'll want to experiment.

Extremities

Hats – Half our body heat goes out our heads. A hat offers warmth and protection from cold and rain, and can block harmful ultraviolet sunrays. When it's cold, you'll want to wear a light wool-knit or fleece toque. In the rain, you'll appreciate a peaked-cap or hood to keep your head reasonably dry. In warm conditions, choose a lightweight cap with breathable mesh for protection against sunburn and heatstroke. To cool down, I enjoy periodically dipping my cap in creek water, or simply dunking my head.

Gloves – These offer warmth and protection for the hands in the event of a wipe out. You want something lightweight, thin, articulated and breathable. I favor mountain biking or cross-country ski gloves.

Accessories

Backpacks – Sometimes you've got to bring a few extras. Running-specific backpacks are small, lightweight and usually feature a hydration system such as a bladder and hose, which allows you to drink while on the run. They sit high on your back and are narrow, allowing you to windmill your arms without chafing. A low profile hip belt and chest strap keep the pack snug. I find an elastic drawstring on the exterior is handy for quick stowing of layers.

Fanny packs – These are low-volume hip-packs perfect for toting the basics such as keys, phone, gloves and dog treats. They're not big enough to hold a bladder, but you can attach a bottle-holster to them or get one designed to hold small rehydration flasks. Be sure it fits your lower back nicely and doesn't bounce when you run.

Headlamps – These are compact flashlights that attach to your head via an elastic strap. They are inexpensive, light and should be carried on adventurous runs or when running near dusk and dawn. Headlamps can be lifesavers and are so small there's no excuse not to pack one.

iPods – An iPod can turn an arctic sloth into a Kenyan track star. While there's no doubt that charging along to your favorite punk rock is highly energizing, be aware that you can't hear animals or mountain bikes that may be sneaking up on you.

LA SPORTIVA®
innovation with passion
www.sportiva.com

FOR **YOUR** MOUNTAIN

FUELLING UP

Food

Avoid digestion-intensive food immediately before and during your run. Try fruit, cereal and yogurt or a light muffin two to three hours before running and save the eggs Benedict for afterwards. If you run first thing in the morning, you should consume something soft and easily absorbed like a banana. Don't head out on an empty stomach, though, or you'll run out of steam.

On most runs lasting an hour or less the body can draw enough energy from muscle stores, but on longer missions you'll need to intake small portions of quick-burst carbohydrates to maintain energy and replace electrolytes. Scientifically engineered nibbles such as gels, shot blocks and energy bars are popular, but be sure to drink water with these or you'll puke! On adventures lasting more than three hours, you may want real food such as gorp, hard sausage, jerky or bagels – stuff with salt, fat and protein. In general, the key is to consume small doses to alleviate cramps or an upset stomach.

Fuelling Up *Is coffee an integral part of a runners morning preparation? It's up to you to decide...*

Hydration

Good hydration is essential for optimal performance and injury prevention. We all know that well-hydrated muscles and ligaments are stronger and suppler. We also know that personal requirements vary dramatically. Be sure to drink plenty of fluids before and after running. Experts suggest replenishing one cup of water for every 15 minutes of exercise. Many runners consume sports-oriented drink mixes that contain carbohydrates and electrolytes to assist in recovery. Popular brands include Refresh, Nuun, Cytomax and Gatorade.

Out in the mountains it can be tempting to drink from creeks and streams. Don't do it! Water-born pathogens such as *Giardia* will reap havoc with your stomach. Avoid gastrointestinal grief by purifying all creek water with a product such as Pristine. Problem is, this procedure is inconvenient when running. If you think you'll need water during your run, it's best to get it from a reliable source and bring it with you in a handheld bottle or bladder-backpack.

A debate regarding the pros and cons of caffeine (street name: coffee) and it's affect on athletic performance continues to rage. Read all you like, but my research suggests that a strong cup of "Black Death" in the form of espresso or Americano is *guaranteed* to supercharge weary trail runners, especially at the crack of dawn. If you enjoy coffee compulsively, I recommend avoiding milk, soy or sugar-injected models such as lattes, café mochas or cappuccinos until *after* your workout, at which point this exotic liquid will taste pleasantly illegal alongside your Belgian waffles.

Rich's Bison Burgers

Ingredients

Organic bison or buffalo sirloin, rolled oats, egg, bread crumbs, jalapeno pepper, garlic, sea salt, portobello mushrooms, black olives, red onions, cilantro

Preparation

- Preheat BBQ to 400 degrees
- Crack a cold beer
- Knead ingredients together and make patties about 1" thick
- Cook 4-6 minutes per side
- Garnish with Colby or jack cheddar
- Add your favorite fixings

Rich's Breakfast Boilers

Ingredients

Cobb's cape-seed loaf, avocado, organic eggs, cheddar cheese, Tabasco sauce

Preparation

- Boil egg (8 minutes)
- Melt cheese on two slices toast
- Cut egg into slices and place over toast
- Slice avocado and lay atop the eggs
- Add Tabasco, salt & cracked black pepper
- Top with second slice of toast
- Devour

Get hooked on trail running

CLINICS

Mountain Madness hosts 4 trail running clinics: meet other trail runners, get to know the trails, learn technique, get your butt out the door, run the race. There's 3 levels related to distance goals and there's many pace groups. Check out the Clinics/Runs page for winter, spring, summer or fall clinics held on Saturday mornings.

"I just wanted to thank you for a fabulous clinic. What a great time we all had. I'm hooked on trail running."

RACES

DIRTY DUO Trail and Mountain Bike race in March in North Vancouver. Gruelling trail race on lower Mount Seymour. Run or ride or do both. www.dirtyduo.com

FAT DOG 100 ultra trail race and relay in July in Manning Park. Demanding race in spectacular scenery. www.mountainmadness.ca/fatdog.php

PHANTOM RUN in November in North Vancouver. This season ender is just an excuse to have a feast and do some fundraising for Save Your Skin Foundation. www.mountainmadness.ca/phantom.php

Mountain Madness races are part of the *Run the North Shore* series.

info@mountainmadness.ca

Photo: Simon Chester *fotographique*

WWW.MOUNTAINMADNESS.CA

Mountain Madness
TRAIL RUNNING

RUNNING TECHNIQUE

Trail running builds coordination, balance, strength and agility, and works more muscle groups than road running. Good posture is important but difficult to maintain on rough, uneven terrain. Try to keep your head up and your eyes focused on the ground several feet ahead. Look for the line of least resistance and focus on where you want to step – your body will follow naturally. The following tips will help you negotiate common terrain obstacles and surfaces:

Hills

When running uphill, shorten your stride and lean forward a touch. Keep your feet underneath your body and your arms relaxed and swinging for momentum. On really steep trails you might use you hands to push off your knees or claw at terrain features. If the effort sends your heart rate through the ceiling there's no shame in walking. In fact, many runners recover by walking hilly sections.

Downhill running can be exciting and fast, but also a little dicey. Over-striding and out-of-control pounding is an injury waiting to happen. It's best to make short, quick strides and avoid sudden braking. Raise your arms a little and widen them for balance.

Streams & Creeks

Stream crossings typically involve small footbridges that may be slippery, loose and occasionally in a state of disrepair. Deluxe models boast chicken wire or grip tape that gives traction. If there's no bridge, stepping-stones or fallen logs may be used, but beware as these can be slick and treacherous. Test all foot placements before committing.

Streams and creeks swell exponentially during heavy rain or spring run-off and may become extra hazardous in these conditions. Steep streams can morph into waterfalls and creeks may become whitewater cauldrons. Be sure to research current trail conditions.

Mud & Puddles

Expect lots of mud all year. Lace your shoes securely to avoid losing them in the slop. Try to stay on the trail as detouring around puddles and mud contributes to erosion. Be especially cautious when striking the ground at angles, such as when rounding a corner.

Roots & Rocks

Vancouver trails are often packed with root systems that are complex and look like anaconda-sized varicose veins. They'll trip you up with the slightest lapse in focus and can be super slick. Treat rocks with equal respect. The worst are loose "baby heads" that appear to be snug in place, but roll out from under you with the first bearing of weight. Slow down in such messy terrain and raise your feet slightly higher than normal to avoid a wipeout.

Ten Trail Tips

- ☐ Start out on easy trails and slowly progress to tougher ones.
- ☐ Always carry a map and know the route you plan to run.
- ☐ Keep your eyes on the trail, generally a body length ahead.
- ☐ Slow and steady wins the race. Wind sprinting will exhaust you in the long run.
- ☐ Always tell someone where you are going and when you plan to return.
- ☐ On runs lasting more than an hour, carry water and snacks.
- ☐ Breathe evenly, relax and go with the flow.
- ☐ Run with a buddy.
- ☐ Power walking is part of the game.
- ☐ Be prepared with appropriate clothing and gear.

Stairs & Boardwalks

Most trails feature some man-made structures. Bridges, staircases and boardwalks are common, and without grip tape or chicken wire, they will be extra slippery. Steps are often widely spaced, making them awkward to run. Be cautious on all structures and use handrails where provided.

Talus & Scree

Talus fields are terrain pockets strewn with massive, loosely stacked boulders that are often jagged and coated in slick moss or lichen. Walk carefully through talus fields to avoid getting maimed and don't be afraid to use your hands for balance.

Scree is basically the same thing but the rocks are way smaller. Think sharp, angular pebbles. Experienced runners like to "boot ski" down scree, but this sketchy technique is best left to deranged mountain goats and nimble hermits.

Snow & Ice

A light dusting of early season snow can be a pleasant novelty, but with a heavy snowpack, trail running becomes sketchy and extremely difficult. Bridges are usually covered with a ridge of ice or hard-packed snow that takes ages to melt. Beware of post-holing, which happens when the snow beneath your foot placement suddenly gives way and you plunge deeply into the abyss. Avoid steep trails and consider carrying a light set of hiking crampons or snowshoes.

CROSS-TRAINING

Now and again it's wise to mix things up to avoid repetitive strain injuries and burnout. The following activities compliment running nicely and are worthy pursuits in their own right:

Cycling

Cycling is excellent leg, cardiovascular and core training, and a fun alternative to trail running. In fact, many of the trails documented in this book have helped cement the status of the North Shore as a mountain biking Shangri-La and this area has truly become the gold standard on which to cut your teeth as a modern-day mountain biker. Road cycling is also very popular in Vancouver and there are many options for spandex-circuits should you desire the tarmac instead.

Yoga

The stronger and more flexible we are, the more force our bodies can absorb. Yoga focuses on mental calmness and controlled breathing as you flow through a series of poses. It improves flexibility, balance, posture, strength and focused breath. In Vancouver, the number of yoga studios rivals that of coffee shops… Om!

Cross-training *Snowshoeing in the Mount Seymour backcountry on a gorgeous winter day.*

Pilates

Pilates involves performing a series of exercises in flow, much like yoga. The difference is that it focuses more on your body's core and is largely apparatus based, which allows you to vary the intensity. Pilates is a low-impact activity that can help rehabilitate strains and knee/lower back issues while improving balance, agility and coordination.

Swimming

Swimming may well be the lowest impact, best overall conditioning activity on the market. It works the entire body, especially the arms and legs. Try running laps around the shallow end of the pool – it's like running in quicksand! Swimming maintains cardiovascular fitness and helps heal running-related injuries. Besides, who can resist a little water polo or a dip in the hot tub?

Weight Training

Weight training will help you achieve a stronger, more balanced body. Pumping iron might not be your cup of tea, but running puts extreme stress on the body, so increasing strength and bone resiliency is a productive strategy. You'll find power beneficial when tackling steep terrain or negotiating technical obstacles such as downed trees.

Snowshoeing

To maintain running fitness during winter, try snowshoeing. A snowshoe is a shovel-like platform that gets strapped to your boot. It keeps you afloat in the powder and provides grip on icy slopes. Snowshoeing is a great workout and the local ski hills have designated snowshoe trails. There are also community events and snowshoe races that cater to the running community. For more information, check out www.theyeti.ca.

Training Instruments

Stopwatches – This is a basic, inexpensive timepiece that accurately records time based on instant activation and de-activation with the press of a single button. Good stopwatches have several functions and can record multiple lap times as well as accumulated time overall. This is the most common tool used by runners and nearly every basic digital watch has a stopwatch feature.

Heart Rate Monitors – Heart rate monitors consist of a sensor/transmitter that is strapped to the chest and a wrist-mounted receiver. These training devices monitor your heart rate so you can determine when to push hard or slow down relative to your energy levels and training goals. Some of these devices can record and plot data for future study, graphing and training strategies.

Pedometers - These devices are simple step counters used to measure distance. Before use, a pedometer must be calibrated for average stride length. It then counts each step based on motion detection. The variable nature of trail terrain (which radically alters the stride) means pedometers aren't totally reliable, but they're an inexpensive option relative to a GPS unit.

When you run consistently you quickly gain fitness and begin to push your mileage and speed boundaries. In the process, you become increasingly susceptible to injuries such as strained muscles, tight illiotibial (IT) bands, patellofemoral syndrome, shin splints, or simply burnout – all of which can shut you down. To prevent this stuff from happening, be sure to warm up and cool down properly. Of course we all want to go farther and feel stronger. That's what's addictive! But if you don't prepare and nurture the body, you risk hitting a wall.

Don't go too hard too soon! When building endurance, increase mileage by no more than 10 percent per week. After 4–5 weeks of "building", adopt a week of rest during which you tone down activity by 15–20 percent. This helps maintain newly acquired fitness but gives joints and muscles a bit of a breather.

Warming up

Warming up gets blood flowing and muscles firing without shocking the musculoskeletal system. Try starting your run as a fast walk for 10–15 minutes, then progress to running when it feels natural. Since it's risky to stretch cold muscles, save stretching for après running when you're fully warmed up.

Cooling Down

At the end of your run don't just stop; slow down to a brisk walk for 10 minutes or so and let your heart rate drop gradually. Why? If you stop abruptly your body dumps lactic acid into your muscles making you stiff and sore. When you cool down gradually you maintain blood flow, which helps to flush lactic acid. This means a more limber body and a faster recovery.

Stretching

Stretching elongates and relaxes muscles leaving you more flexible, agile and stronger. Ease into a stretch to a threshold of mild tension. Breathe as you hold the position until tension subsides. Do not bounce or force a stretch. If tension increases you should back off. Build the stretch over 30–45 seconds or more. Trail running is obviously lower-body oriented so, when stretching, runners should focus on hamstrings, quadriceps, IT bands, calves, hip flexors, lower back muscles and the groin.

Balance & Stability

Balance and stability is very important since trails are often uneven, and the risk of ankle sprains or knee injuries is omnipresent. Strengthening these joints by standing on a wobble board or inflatable rubber "pancake" is highly effective, as is weight training or a balance-oriented activity like yoga. For appropriate personal exercises, you should consult a physiotherapist.

CLIMATE & WEATHER

The south coast of British Columbia has the mildest climate in Canada and areas under 1,000 m (3,000 ft) rarely see temperatures dip below zero degrees Celsius. The terrain is predominantly rainforest and it's true that biblical downpours can hammer the city, but all that moisture simply keeps the landscape lush and vibrant.

Vancouver also gets its share of warm stable weather, mostly during the summer months. July and August are typically hot and dry, and occasionally bring moderate drought conditions. September is very pleasant with stable sunny weather and cool breezes that hint of autumn. October through April is the rainy season, with January and February bringing winter and the greatest likelihood of low-lying snow. It's rare to get snow in the city, but it does happen.

The North Shore mountains are a different story: they often generate a local weather system and it's not uncommon for the city to be sunny when the North Shore mountains are engulfed in a dark, threatening stew of precipitation. These mountains gather an average annual snowfall of about 400 cm in the alpine (above 1,000 m), which is great for skiers and snowshoers, but not so good for trail runners. The good news is that most of the trails are in the forest below alpine so year-round running is the norm.

Impending Doom *Summer evening storm clouds gather directly above the high rises of downtown Vancouver.*

Daylight

Vancouver sits in the Northern Hemisphere at a latitude of 49° 11' N and a longitude of 123° 10' W. Daylight values fluctuate widely throughout the year. The following are daily averages in hours for each month:

January	8:17
February	9:25
March	11:00
April	12:53
May	14:36
June	15:57
July	16:10
August	15:08
September	13:28
October	11:40
November	9:52
December	8:29

Weather Forecasts

Seven-day forecasts may be obtained on the Environment Canada website, Weatheroffice.gc.ca, by navigating to the province of British Columbia and then the city forecast of your choice.

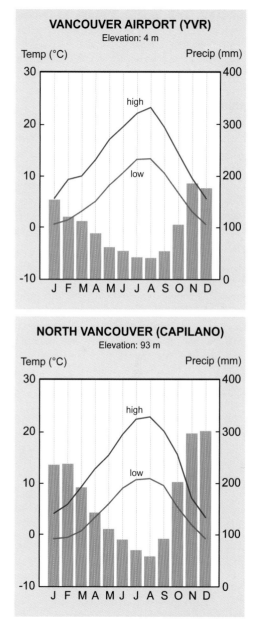

Figure 1 *Average monthly precipitation and temperature for Vancouver and North Vancouver. Note the higher precipitation values for the North Vancouver Capilano weather station, which is nestled at the base of the North Shore mountains.*

HOW TO USE THIS BOOK

This guidebook is the ultimate reference for Vancouver trail runners and a wealth of information is provided for each running circuit. Take a moment to educate yourself on the nuances of the run descriptions – it will pay dividends when attempting a run for the first time.

Run Overview

To help you choose an appropriate workout, each run is assigned a variety of key icons and statistics. The **difficulty code** tells you how technical the route is. The **run number** helps you locate the circuit on a corresponding detailed map. The heart-shaped **burl factor** icons hint at how strenuous or hilly the run will be. The total **distance** (car to car) is provided in kilometres. Underneath the run name is a list of **run statistics**. From left to right, these are: elevation *change* (lowest point on trail to highest), typical months the route is snow-free and GPS coordinates for the trailhead. Underneath the run statistics is a brief paragraph or two describing what to expect from each circuit. Following this, **The Dirt** gives detailed directions for following the route in a bullet-point format.

Elevation Graphs

Each trail contains an elevation graph that provides information about the distance of the trail versus the change in elevation. To emphasize relief, a vertical exaggeration of two has been used (i.e., each metre travelled horizontally equals two metres on the vertical axis). Whether you prefer a short, flat jaunt or a steep, marathon of a workout, this should aid in your selection.

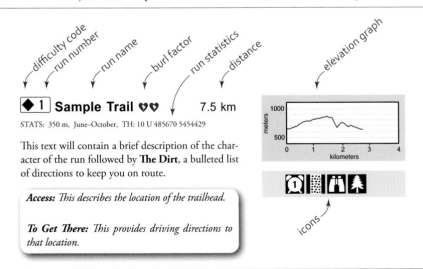

difficulty code — run number — run name — burl factor — run statistics — distance — elevation graph

◆ 1 Sample Trail ♥♥   7.5 km

STATS: 350 m, June–October, TH: 10 U 485670 5454429

This text will contain a brief description of the character of the run followed by **The Dirt**, a bulleted list of directions to keep you on route.

Access: This describes the location of the trailhead.

To Get There: This provides driving directions to that location.

icons

Icons

Each run has a corresponding blue **icon** box with a variety of running-related symbols that provide basic information about the characteristics of the run (see key on right). The clock icon indicates the *estimated* number of hours the run will take from car to car and is rounded up to the nearest quarter hour. Actual run times vary greatly between runners; take this estimate with a grain of salt.

Finding the Trailhead

Each run page contains a yellow box that holds critical information related to finding the trailhead. The *location* of each trailhead is found in the ***Access*** paragraph; the specific *directions* for driving to the trailhead are located in the ***To Get There*** paragraph.

Notes on Difficulty

Any given trail's difficulty is totally subjective. Understand that running 15 kilometres on a flat gravel path is far easier than a five-kilometre battleground of talus, roots and hills. For this reason, the ratings given refer *exclusively to the ground underfoot*. Other factors such as distance, elevation, hill intensity and trail condition must also be considered when choosing a run. I suggest starting with short, less technical circuits and slowly progressing as you gain fitness and confidence. The following ratings are loosely based on the well-known ski difficulty scales:

● 1 **Novice** – May include small obstacles like roots, rocks, potholes, bridges and boardwalks. Hills will be short and gentle. Expect buff paths that are generally well maintained and signed. If you can walk and have decent health, you should be fine.

■ 1 **Intermediate** – Bigger obstacles, possibly including loose debris, downed trees, boulder hopping and natural stream crossings. Be prepared for narrow twisty singletrack, abrupt direction changes, uneven slopes and steep hill climbs. Good fitness is advised.

Icon Key

🕐	Estimated run time
	Paved trail
	Packed gravel trail
	Jogging strollers OK
↑	One way run
↕	Return on same trail
	Run follows a loop
∞	Run is a trail circuit
🍸	Urban setting
	Alpine terrain
	Remote/long run
	Watch for horses
🌲	Giant trees
	Share route with bikes
	Mountain bike hazard
	Close to beach
	Great views
	Waterfall
	No dogs allowed

◆ 1 **Advanced** – These routes dish out a constant barrage of challenging and large obstacles. Man-made structures may be decrepit and covered in "spooge". Steep switchbacks and sudden, dramatic elevation changes are common. Hills are steep, long and frequent. These trails can be difficult to walk on, let alone run. Excellent fitness and stamina recommended.

▲ 1 **Expert** – Expect all of the above over long distances and at alpine elevations. Major hill climbs are guaranteed, as are washouts, storm debris and talus fields. Basic scrambling (use of hands) may be required. Expert trails are rarely maintained and require advanced hiking skills. You'll want strong mountain skills, peak fitness and a full quiver of mountain-running weaponry.

Burl Factor

Each run is also given a "burl" factor rating that is indicative of overall steepness. A run with no hearts will be relatively flat, otherwise, the following apply:

❤   This run is not flat and will require some moderate uphill running.

❤❤   A substantial amount of uphill running is to be expected.

❤❤❤   Uphill running of massive proportions. A prime example is the *Grouse Grind*.

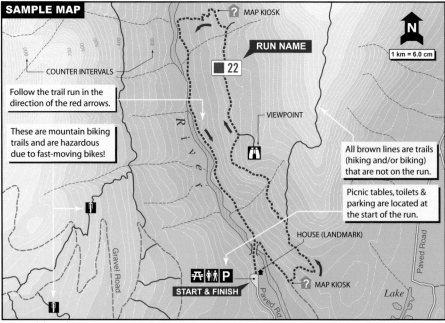

Trails

All trails in this book were mapped with a Garmin Map-60CX handheld GPS unit. Universal Transverse Mercator (UTM) coordinates have been given for trailhead locations (note that the UTM zone designation for all runs in this guide is: 10 U). These maps are detailed and invaluable, so learn how to read and interpret them!

Please note there are many trails out there NOT INCLUDED on these maps. Mountain bike trails that are included are labeled with a tire icon. All the running circuit trails are depicted in red, orange or purple. All other trails (including mountain bike trails) are depicted in brown.

Contour Maps

All the trails in this book are represented on contour maps to provide a general overview of the land along with any prominent features. These contour maps contain white lines (the contours) that show detailed undulations in the terrain. The contours are labelled in metres and, for the experienced user, this can provide information about the steepness and nature of each run. Each map also contains a directional arrow that points to north and a small scale key to help approximate distances between points on the map.

The sample map on the left has notes on general map use and the adjacent map key lists the main features on the maps along with an example of each feature.

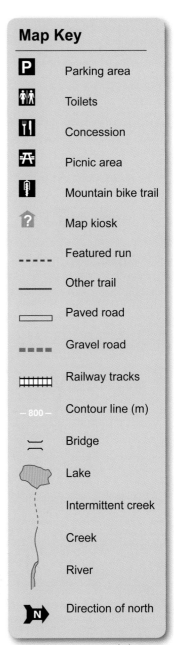

Map Key

P	Parking area
	Toilets
	Concession
	Picnic area
	Mountain bike trail
?	Map kiosk
- - - - -	Featured run
_____	Other trail
	Paved road
- - - -	Gravel road
	Railway tracks
— 800 —	Contour line (m)
	Bridge
	Lake
	Intermittent creek
	Creek
	River
N	Direction of north

Vancouver *The city, with the downtown core on the left, as seen from the North Shore mountains*

CHAPTER 1:

VANCOUVER

Spread across the cosmopolitan city of Vancouver is an abundance of relatively tame trails perfect for runners seeking civilized, quick-hit workouts. All runs are easily accessible from nearby neighbourhoods and feature not only forested singletrack trails, but also significant mileage along beachfront pathways.

VANCOUVER TRAIL RUNNING ZONES

1 Pacific Spirit Park

Pacific Spirit Park comprises over 750 hectares of forest and foreshore that stretches across the Point Grey peninsula on Vancouver's West Side. The park sits adjacent to the University of British Columbia (UBC) and contains over 75 kilometres of relatively gentle trails that are mostly packed gravel, well-signed and doable year-round.

The predominantly upland forest plateau yields mostly flat trails, but steep ravines and hillsides drop abruptly to surrounding beaches. At low tide, these beaches reveal large tidal flats that are great for running barefoot.

2 Stanley Park

Stanley Park sits smack in the middle of Vancouver at the head of the downtown peninsula between English Bay and Vancouver Harbour. It's the oldest park in the city and one of Vancouver's main tourist attractions. Inside, you'll discover a wealth of gentle trails meandering throughout 400 hectares of impressive evergreen forest. The park is rich with natural history and bursting with wildlife. It's also full of monuments and iconic landmarks including Lost Lagoon, Siwash Rock, Prospect Point and Beaver Lake. Runners will enjoy the tranquillity of the forested trails as well as the world-famous seawall that circumnavigates the park.

3 False Creek

False Creek is a short inlet that leads from English Bay into the heart of Vancouver immediately south of the downtown core. Marked by the Burrard Street Bridge at the west end and Science World to the east, False Creek brims with lifestyle-focused residents and recreational users. Of interest to runners is the continuous paved path lining the waterfront that is traffic-free and ripe with coastal ambience. You'll typically see kayaks and yachts cruising the water alongside small urban parks, trendy apartment complexes and the artsy shopping quarter of Granville Island. Bring your yoga mat.

Vancouver *An inukshuk (stone landmark of Inuit origin) rests on the point by English Bay beach park (right) and a stunning overview of the seawall from the Burrard Street bridge (far right).*

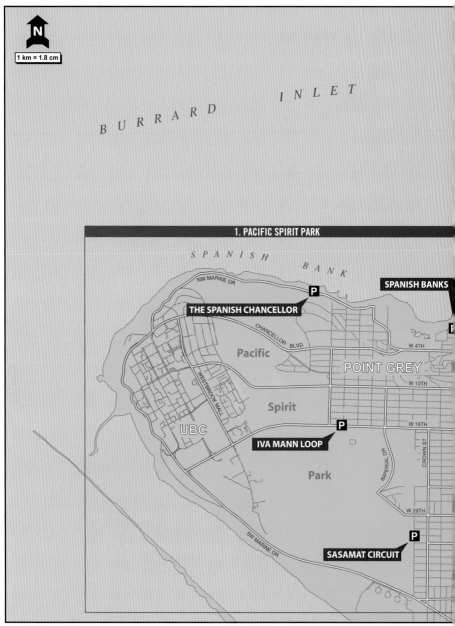

N

1 km = 1.8 cm

BURRARD INLET

1. PACIFIC SPIRIT PARK

SPANISH BANK

NW MARINE DR

THE SPANISH CHANCELLOR

CHANCELLOR BLVD

Pacific

W 4TH

POINT GREY

W 10TH

WESTBROOK MALL

Spirit

W 16TH

UBC

IVA MANN LOOP

IMPERIAL DR

CROWN ST

Park

W 29TH

SW MARINE DR

SASAMAT CIRCUIT

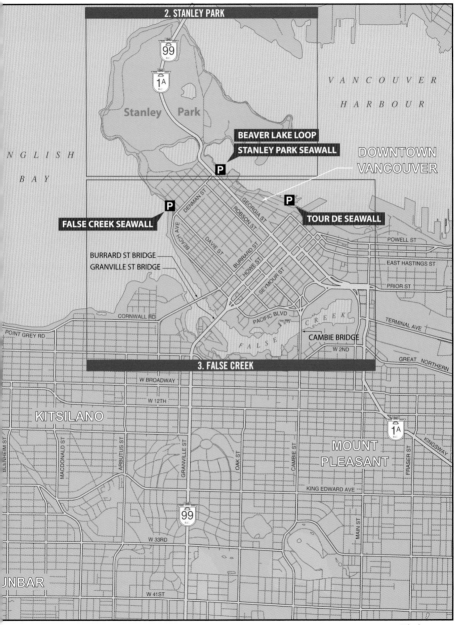

2. STANLEY PARK

99 B.C.

1 A B.C.

Stanley Park

VANCOUVER

HARBOUR

BEAVER LAKE LOOP
STANLEY PARK SEAWALL

DOWNTOWN
VANCOUVER

NGLISH

BAY

P

P

FALSE CREEK SEAWALL

TOUR DE SEAWALL

DENMAN ST
ROBSON ST
GEORGIA ST

POWELL ST

BEACH AVE
DAVIE ST
BURRARD ST
HOWE ST
SEYMOUR ST

EAST HASTINGS ST

PRIOR ST

BURRARD ST BRIDGE
GRANVILLE ST BRIDGE

CORNWALL RD

PACIFIC BLVD

CREEK

TERMINAL AVE

POINT GREY RD

CAMBIE BRIDGE

W 2ND

FALSE

GREAT NORTHERN

3. FALSE CREEK

W BROADWAY

W 12TH

KITSILANO

1 A B.C.

BLENHEIM ST
MACDONALD ST
ARBUTUS ST
GRANVILLE ST
OAK ST
CAMBIE ST

MOUNT
PLEASANT

FRASER ST
KINGSWAY

KING EDWARD AVE

99 B.C.

MAIN ST

W 33RD

JNBAR

W 41ST

● 1 The Spanish Chancellor   5.1 km

STATS: 227 m, Year-round, TH: 10 U 483666 5458308

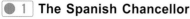

This run explores several prominent trails in the northern portion of Pacific Spirit Park above historic Spanish Banks. En route, you'll dip in and out of a large, lush canyon and pass by an interesting swamp. It's a pleasant introduction to singletrack trail running with minimal hill climbing and lots of potential for variations.

The Dirt

▶ From the parking lot at Spanish Banks Creek, cross the road to a map kiosk. Run *Spanish* for 50 m and turn RIGHT on *Admiralty*.

▶ Keep RIGHT along the path high above the beach to a signed junction with *East Canyon*. Stay RIGHT and descend to the canyon floor before climbing steeply up the other side to a junction with *West Canyon* (sign).

▶ Continue RIGHT along *Admiralty*, past a short exit trail to Northwest Marine Drive, to a junction with *Salish* (sign). Turn LEFT and head up *Salish* to the University Hill Elementary school. Keep RIGHT and run along the road to the traffic lights at Chancellor Boulevard.

▶ Cross Chancellor Boulevard and re-enter *Salish*. Stay LEFT past *Sword Fern* and run to a junction with *Spanish* (sign). Turn LEFT and descend *Spanish*, keeping LEFT past an unmarked three-way junction to a picturesque swamp.

▶ Continue past the swamp to a junction with *Pioneer* (sign). Turn LEFT on *Pioneer* and run to Chancellor Boulevard. Cross Chancellor Boulevard and re-enter the forest on *Pioneer*. Run 10 m and turn RIGHT onto *Chancellor* (unmarked).

▶ At an unmarked three-way junction, turn LEFT and descend a trail, keeping RIGHT past *Pioneer* and *Admiralty* junctions, to Spanish Banks beach and parking area.

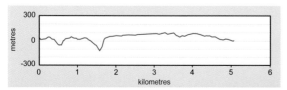

www.quickdrawpublications.com

Access: Start at the Spanish Banks Creek parking lot.

To Get There: From Route 99 (Granville Street), head west along West Broadway. Turn RIGHT on Arbutus Street, then LEFT on West 4th Avenue. Head past Jericho Beach Park (on the right) to traffic lights and a junction with NW Marine Drive. Turn RIGHT and drive 2.3 km, passing Locarno Beach and Spanish Banks. Look for a white sign with a yellow fish that says "Spanish Banks Creek" and turn RIGHT into the parking area. Opposite is an obvious trailhead and map kiosk.

Map: Pages 54–55

Variation: Start The Spanish Chancellor by running west along *Admiralty*. At *East Canyon,* go LEFT and follow it uphill, staying right past several junctions. Eventually, descend *West Canyon* to reconnect with *Admiralty* and the remainder of The Spanish Chancellor. This excellent side trip adds 1.5 km. Want more? Simply cruise the beachfront as far as you like, either before or after running The Spanish Chancellor.

The Spanish Chancellor *Downtown Vancouver in evening light as seen from the parking area at Point Grey Beach.*

2 Spanish Banks   10.6 km

STATS: 84 m, Year-round, TH: 10 U 486347 5457744

This low-key ramble cruises a playful beachfront, spanning Jericho Beach, Locarno Beach and Spanish Banks, to the Pacific Spirit Park boundary. It returns along *Admiralty*, which follows a forested bench above the beach with sensational views over Georgia Strait and Burrard Inlet. *Admiralty* leads to *East Canyon* and *West Canyon*, which both follow loamy singletrack up and down a deep, lush gully. These are amongst the most technical trails in Pacific Spirit Park and the canyon vistas are unique.

The Dirt

▶ From the Hastings Mill Museum Park, run west along Cornwall Avenue for 250 m to Jericho Beach Park. You'll pass by the Royal Vancouver Yacht Club, Jericho Tennis Club and Brock House Seniors Center, all on your right.

▶ Enter Jericho Beach Park, pass the toilets and concession on the right and begin running along the wide gravel path by the waterfront. Follow this for 1 km to the Jericho Sailing Club. ▶▶

Access: *The trailhead is on Point Grey Road near Jericho Beach.*

To Get There: *From Route 99 (Granville Street), head west on West Broadway for about 3 km to Alma Street. Turn RIGHT and drive nine blocks north to Point Grey Road. Turn LEFT and look for parking around the Hastings Mill Museum Park at the bottom of Alma Street. The large grass field found here is a great place for a pre-run stretch.*

Map: *Pages 54–55*

▶ Continue along the gravel path, past Locarno Beach and Spanish Banks Beach, to an off-leash dog area at Point Grey Beach. Continue running until the path ends at Northwest Marine Drive. At this point, locate a small roadside trail and follow it for 300 m to Pacific Spirit Regional Park entrance, which consists of a parking lot and toilets.

▶ Cross the road to *Admiralty*. Jump onto the trail and immediately turn LEFT. Run *Admiralty* along a bench above the beach for 800 m. At a junction (sign) turn RIGHT and run up *West Canyon* for 800 m to a junction with *East Canyon* (sign).

▶ Turn LEFT and head back toward the beachfront. The trail meanders a little before crossing a bridge. Keep left alongside the canyon, tightly contouring a long fence. Continue down to a junction with *Admiralty* and turn LEFT. Descend 100 m to a junction in a creek drainage and exit RIGHT toward Northwest Marine Drive.

▶ Cross the road and run across the field to the beachfront path. Turn RIGHT and retrace your steps back to Jericho Beach Park.

> **Variation:** For an alternate finish, run east past the Jericho Sailing Club for 400 m and, at an obvious fork, go RIGHT for about 200 m toward the duck ponds. At the ponds, turn LEFT and take the trail directly to Cornwall Avenue and back to your car.

Spanish Banks *Clockwise from left: Lush vegetation on East Canyon Trail; Fun for everyone on West Canyon Trail; please obey canine etiquette!*

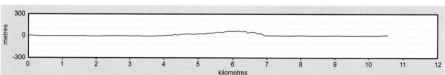

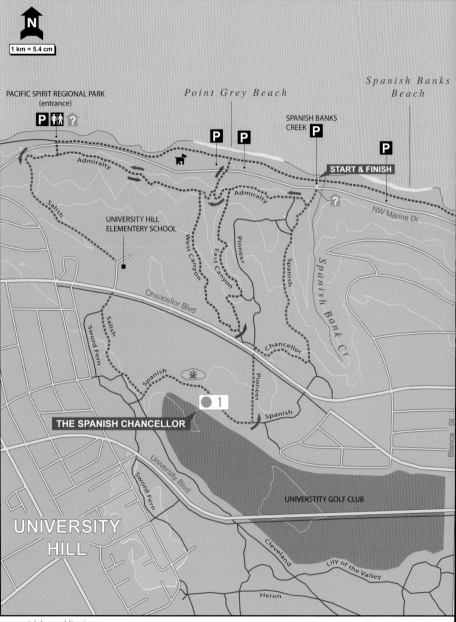

N
1 km = 5.4 cm

PACIFIC SPIRIT REGIONAL PARK
(entrance)

Point Grey Beach

Spanish Banks Beach

SPANISH BANKS CREEK

START & FINISH

Admiralty

Admiralty

NW Marine Dr

Salish

UNIVERSITY HILL ELEMENTERY SCHOOL

West Canyon

East Canyon

Pioneer

Spanish

Spanish Bank Cr

Chancellor Blvd

Salish

Sword Fern

Spanish

Chancellor

Pioneer

THE SPANISH CHANCELLOR

1

Spanish

Blanca St

University Blvd

Sword Fern

UNIVERSITY HILL

UNIVERSTITY GOLF CLUB

Cleveland

Lily of the Valley

Heron

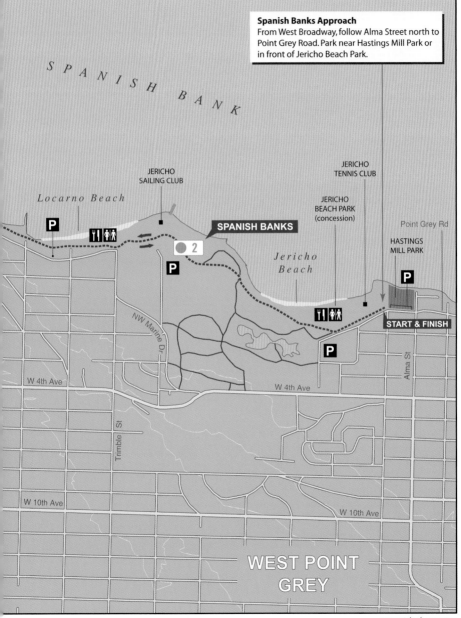

Spanish Banks Approach
From West Broadway, follow Alma Street north to Point Grey Road. Park near Hastings Mill Park or in front of Jericho Beach Park.

SPANISH BANK

JERICHO SAILING CLUB

JERICHO TENNIS CLUB

JERICHO BEACH PARK (concession)

Point Grey Rd

Locarno Beach

SPANISH BANKS

HASTINGS MILL PARK

2

Jericho Beach

START & FINISH

NW Marine Dr

W 4th Ave

W 4th Ave

Alma St

Trimble St

W 10th Ave

W 10th Ave

WEST POINT GREY

3 Iva Mann Loop 7.5 km

STATS: 93 m, Year-round, TH: 10 U 484427 5456165

This fun little rip cruises wide, flat, easy-to-follow paths with excellent signage typical of Pacific Spirit Park. The forest is beautiful, especially along *Lily of the Valley* where you'll pass some impressive trees! Several road crossings are mandatory along this run, so use caution on the busy streets. When in doubt, follow the dark-green markers on all signs labeled "Iva Mann Walk". Dog owners take note that part of this route has a dog ban on weekends and statutory holidays.

The Dirt

▶ From West 16th Avenue, head down *Nature* for 800 m to *Hemlock*, passing junctions with *Deer Fern* and *Cleveland* along the way. Turn RIGHT and run 100 m to a junction with *Salish*.

▶ Go RIGHT on *Salish* for 100 m to *Iron Knee*. Turn LEFT down *Iron Knee* and then RIGHT on *Council*.

▶ Run *Council* for 125 m, then turn RIGHT up *Sword Fern*. (The signpost here is poorly marked. It reads like you're turning right on *Council*, but in fact it is *Sword Fern*).

▶ Run *Sword Fern* to a junction with *Salish* (this stretch is a touch "spicy"). Turn LEFT on *Salish* and run 200 m to West 16th Avenue. Go LEFT to a fire hydrant then cross the road to *Salish*.

▶ Turn LEFT, follow a roadside path for 100 m (past a large information sign) to *Sword Fern* and turn RIGHT.

▶ Run *Sword Fern* past *Heron* to University Hill School at Acadia Road. Continue past the school and turn RIGHT on Ortona Avenue.

▶ Run past townhouses for 100 m and turn LEFT onto *Sword Fern*. Follow *Sword Fern* to University Boulevard, passing through a minor intersection with *Fairview*.

▶ Cross University Boulevard and continue on *Sword Fern,* passing two unmarked intersections with *Spanish. Sword Fern* eventually banks right to a junction with *Salish*. ▶▶

Access: Start on the south side of West 16th Avenue, about 100 m east of Blanca Street by a bus stop.

To Get There: From Route 99 (Granville Street), head west toward Point Grey along West 16th Avenue. Drive for 5.5 km to Blanca Street and park

Map: Page 59

Interesting Fact: In 1957, University Endowment Lands resident, Iva Mann, lobbied the provincial government to create Pacific Spirit Regional Park. She volunteered, built trails and served on the Greater Vancouver Regional District board for about 20 years. This route honors her commitment to preserving the University Endowment Lands as a park.

Iva Mann Loop *Gliding along the Nature trail in Pacific Spirit Park, the lush forested lands adjacent to the University of British Columbia.*

Iva Mann Loop *Running amongst some very large trees on Council trail.*

▶ At *Salish,* turn RIGHT and run south past two intersections with *Spanish*. Continue past a golf course (on the left) to University Boulevard.

▶ Cross University Boulevard to a church parking lot. Cruise past clothing donation bins to *Salish*, just right of a brown fence. Run *Salish* for 200 m and turn LEFT onto *Lily of the Valley*.

▶ Follow *Lily of the Valley* for 1 km, across an intersection with *Cleveland*, to a junction with *Vine Maple*. Charge down *Vine Maple* past the *Newt Loop* to Blanca Street. Turn RIGHT toward West 16th Avenue and the finish!

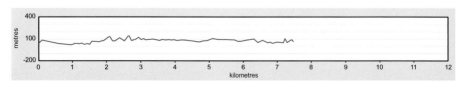

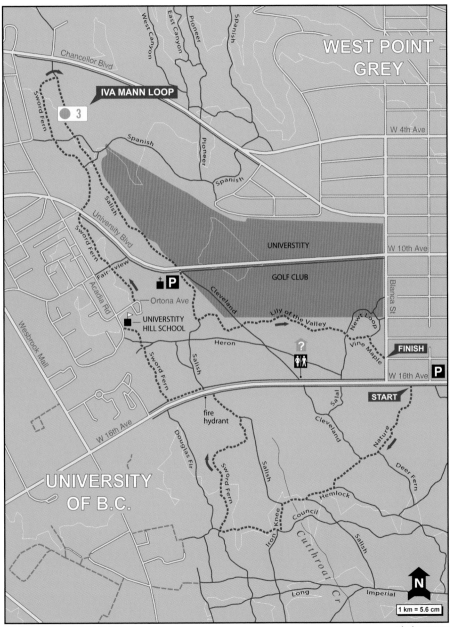

WEST POINT GREY

Chancellor Blvd

West Canyon
East Canyon
Pioneer
Spanish

IVA MANN LOOP

● 3

Sword Fern

Spanish

Pioneer

Spanish

W 4th Ave

Salish

University Blvd

Sword Fern

Fairview

Acadia Rd

UNIVERSTITY

W 10th Ave

GOLF CLUB

Blanca St

P

Ortona Ave

UNIVERSTITY
HILL SCHOOL

Cleveland

Lily of the Valley

Newt Loop

Vine Maple

FINISH

Westbrook Mall

Sword Fern

Salish

Heron

?

W 16th Ave

P

START

fire
hydrant

Douglas Fir

Sword Fern

Salish

Cleveland

Isla

Nature

Deer Fern

UNIVERSITY
OF B.C.

W 16th Ave

Iron Knee

Council

Hemlock

Salish

Cuthroat Cr

Long

Imperial

N

1 km = 5.6 cm

4 Sasamat Circuit

9.7 km

STATS: 93 m, Year-round, TH: 10 U 485670 5454429

Are you craving a fast, easy 10-kilometre run? If so, check out this circuit. It's possible to sprint the entire distance due to the friendly grade and minimal number of obstacles (the trails are mostly wide packed gravel and change very little in elevation). This route explores the southern region of Pacific Spirit Park between West 16th Avenue and Southwest Marine Drive, and is a great run if you want flow *and* mileage without the strain of running gnarly hills.

The Dirt

▶ From West 33rd Avenue and Camosun Street, run down *Sasamat* (past *St. George's*, outhouses and picnic tables) to a junction with *Clinton*. Turn RIGHT and continue up *Sasamat*.

▶ At a junction with *Hemlock,* stay RIGHT and continue up *Sasamat* to *Imperial* (power line). Cross *Imperial* and continue up *Sasamat* to a junction with *Council*. Stay RIGHT on *Sasamat*.

> *Access: The trailhead is at West 33rd Avenue and Camosun Street, near the University of British Columbia (UBC).*
>
> *To Get There: From Route 99 (Granville Street), go west on West 16th Avenue toward UBC. Turn LEFT on Dunbar Street and head south to West 33rd Avenue. Turn RIGHT and drive four blocks to the obvious trailhead and information kiosk at a yellow gate.*
>
> *Map: Page 61*

▶ Run *Sasamat* past a junction with *Huckleberry* to a huge, concrete water reservoir. At the reservoir, go LEFT on *Sasamat*. Continue past *Top* to a service road and go LEFT for 25 m to West 16th Avenue. Turn RIGHT and run 400 m to Imperial Road.

▶ At Imperial Road, turn RIGHT into the forest onto *Huckleberry* and run 450 m to *Top*. Turn LEFT on *Top* and run to Imperial Road.

▶ At Imperial Road, turn RIGHT and run the roadside for 250 m to a yellow gate and info kiosk. Continue past the kiosk on *Imperial* (under the power lines) for 1.5 km. Pass *Hemlock* and *Salish* before reaching an unmarked fork. Stay RIGHT and continue under the power line, passing *Long* and *Iron Knee*, until you reach *Sword Fern*.

▶ Turn LEFT down *Sword Fern*. Run past intersections with *Long* and *Imperial* all the way to Southwest Marine Drive. At Southwest Marine Drive, turn LEFT and run a roadside trail for an endless 1.8 km to an intersection and yellow gate. Make a sharp LEFT onto *Clinton* and quickly veer RIGHT past signs to a junction with *Salish*.

▶ Keep LEFT on *Clinton* and run to an intersection with *Sasamat*. Turn RIGHT on *Sasamat* and run past picnic tables and toilets. Return to West 33rd Avenue and Camosun Street – you're done!

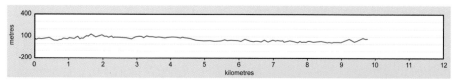

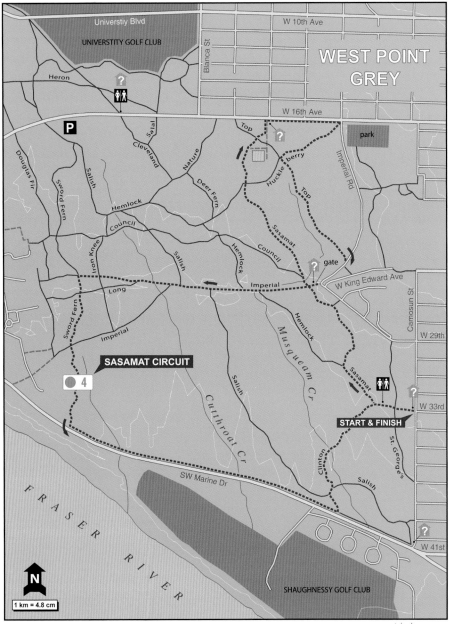

UNIVERSTITY GOLF CLUB

Universtiy Blvd

W 10th Ave

Blanca St

WEST POINT GREY

park

W 16th Ave

Heron

Top

Huckleberry

Top

Imperial Rd

Cleveland

Nature

Deer Fern

Salish

Douglas Fir

Sword Fern

Hemlock

Council

Iron Knee

Salish

Sasamat

Council

Hemlock

gate

Imperial

W King Edward Ave

Long

Hemlock

Camosun St

Imperial

W 29th

Musqueam Cr

Sasamat

SASAMAT CIRCUIT

● 4

Salish

Cutthroat Cr

W 33rd

START & FINISH

St. George's

Clinton

Salish

SW Marine Dr

W 41st

F R A S E R   R I V E R

N

1 km = 4.8 cm

SHAUGHNESSY GOLF CLUB

5 Stanley Park Seawall   10.1 km

STATS: 35 m, Year-round, TH: 10 U 490237 5460070

As the name suggests, the Stanley Park Seawall circumnavigates Vancouver's flagship park via the waterfront and leads past many famous landmarks. As you round the park, this historic pathway gives unrivalled views of Coal Harbour, the North Shore and English Bay. When you reach Third Beach, you might be inspired to run this sandy stretch as a pleasant deviation from the asphalt surface. Plenty of burger stands keep the tourists at bay, but watch out for charging baby strollers!

The Dirt

▶ From the steel sculpture, follow a path north toward the marina for 150 m and veer LEFT onto the primary pedestrian path. Cross a concrete bridge to a large roundabout and information kiosk.

▶ Turn RIGHT and follow the obvious seawall all the way around Stanley Park to Second Beach. Along the way, run past the following landmarks: Vancouver Rowing Club, Totem Poles, Nine O'clock Gun, Brockton Point Lighthouse, Empress of Japan, Girl in Wetsuit (a statue in the ocean), Lions Gate Bridge, Siwash Rock (a sea stack) and Third Beach.

▶ When you reach Second Beach, turn LEFT just before the swimming pool then turn RIGHT toward the concession stand. Immediately past the concession stand, turn LEFT and cross the road. Continue on the paved path for 400 m to a junction and go RIGHT across a bridge.

▶ Continue STRAIGHT along the main pathway around Lost Lagoon to a tunnel leading under West Georgia Street. Go through the tunnel to an information kiosk and roundabout, and continue STRAIGHT for 200 m to a fork.

▶ Turn RIGHT and run 150 m back to the steel sculpture at Denman and West Georgia streets.

Access: Begin at the northwest corner of West Georgia and Denman streets (Route 99/1A). Look for a large steel sculpture opposite the Running Room.

To Get There: From Downtown, drive northwest on Route 99/1A (West Georgia Street), and look for parking near the corner of Denman and West Georgia Street.

Map: Pages 66-67

Stanley Park Seawall *Clockwise from right: Seawall from Lion's Gate Bridge; Statue of 1912 Canadian Track & Field star, Harry Jerome; Seawall near Siwash Rock.*

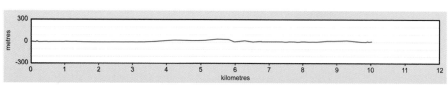

● 6 Beaver Lake Loop   6.9 km
STATS: 60 m, Year-round, TH: 10 U 490237 5460070

This nice run circumnavigates tranquil Beaver Lake and follows gorgeous, forested pathways lined with enormous, old-growth trees. The loop also provides a glimpse of the epic devastation Stanley Park suffered in December, 2006, when a major winter storm with hurricane force winds roared through the groves, leveling an estimated 10,000 massive trees and obliterating major sections of the seawall.

Access: Start as for the Stanley Park Seawall run at the large steel sculpture opposite the Running Room.

Map: Pages 66–67

The Dirt

▶ From the steel sculpture, follow the paved path toward the marina and merge LEFT onto the primary pedestrian path which travels alongside the water.

▶ Quickly cross a concrete bridge to a large roundabout and information kiosk. Turn RIGHT and take the central paved path over a wide concrete bridge (NOT the seawall path).

▶ At the statue of Lord Stanley, turn LEFT and cross Pipeline Road. Immediately trend RIGHT, follow a paved path for 75 m and go LEFT through a garden to *South Creek.* ▶▶

Beaver Lake Loop *Clockwise from left: Lily pads frame the calm waters of Beaver Lake; sprinting past Lost Lagoon; massive trees along Cathedral Trail.*

▶ Head up *South Creek* and keep LEFT at the first unmarked fork. At a junction with *Wren,* turn RIGHT toward Beaver Lake. After 150 m, turn RIGHT and run counterclockwise around Beaver Lake for 600 m, past *Tisdall* and *Ravine,* to a junction with *Lake.*

▶ Turn RIGHT on *Lake* and run to a pedestrian overpass crossing the Stanley Park Causeway (Route 99). After the overpass, turn RIGHT on *Bridle Path,* run past *Thompson* and go LEFT on *Rawlings.*

▶ Follow *Rawlings* across an intersection with *Thompson.* A little further, keep LEFT past *Raccoon* (unmarked). Follow *Rawlings* to a meadow with the iconic Hollow Tree, a massive Western redcedar with a car-sized hole in the base.

▶ Continue down *Rawlings* past *Lake* and turn LEFT on *Tatlow.* Run past *Lovers Walk* and turn RIGHT on *Bridle Path.*

▶ Run to a large intersection with a shelter, head down *Cathedral* (between the shelter and a fire hydrant) and cruise through the devastated forest. Cross North Lagoon Drive to a paved path and continue over a bridge to a junction with a paved foot and bike path.

▶ Turn LEFT and take the gravel trail tightly around Lost Lagoon. Beware of the aggressive swans! After about 500 m, reach some toilets. Veer LEFT and run through the tunnel leading under West Georgia Street.

▶ Continue STRAIGHT through the map kiosk and roundabout and cross the concrete bridge. Go a short distance to a fork and go RIGHT back to the steel sculpture at Denman and West Georgia streets.

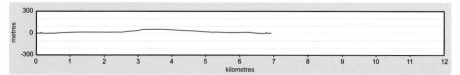

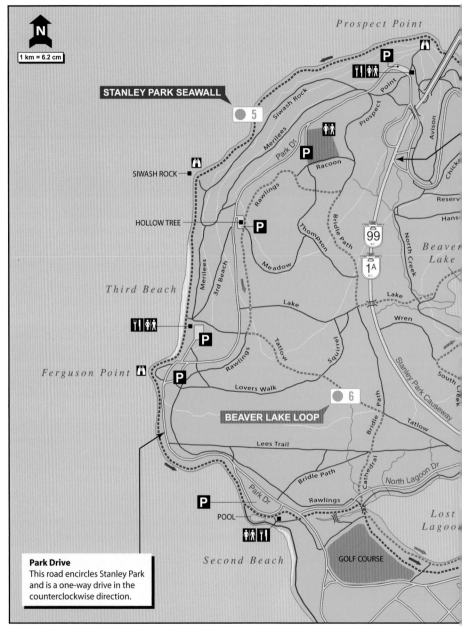

N

1 km = 6.2 cm

Prospect Point

STANLEY PARK SEAWALL

● 5

SIWASH ROCK

HOLLOW TREE

Third Beach

Ferguson Point

● 6

BEAVER LAKE LOOP

POOL

Second Beach

Siwash Rock

Park Dr.

Prospect Point

Avison

Racoon

Merilees

Rawlings

Thompson

Bridle Path

Meadow

3rd Beach

Merilees

Lake

Lake

Tatlow

Rawlings

Squirrel

Lovers Walk

Bridle Path

Stanley Park Causeway

South Creek

North Creek

Beaver Lake

Reserv

Hans

Wren

Chick

Lees Trail

Bridle Path

Cathedral

Tatlow

North Lagoon Dr

Park Dr

Rawlings

GOLF COURSE

Lost Lagoon

99
B.C.

1A
B.C.

Park Drive
This road encircles Stanley Park and is a one-way drive in the counterclockwise direction.

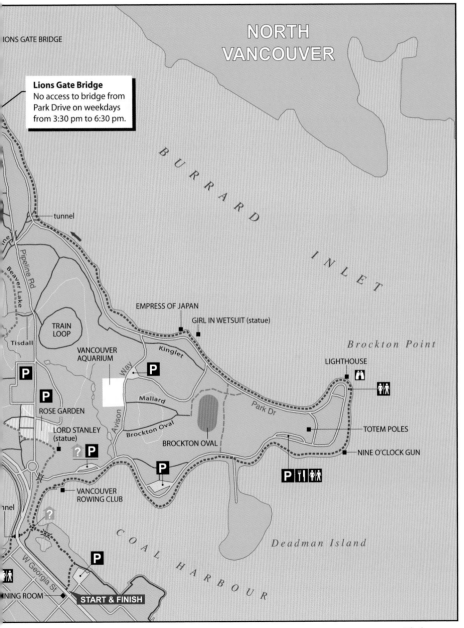

NORTH
VANCOUVER

IONS GATE BRIDGE

Lions Gate Bridge
No access to bridge from
Park Drive on weekdays
from 3:30 pm to 6:30 pm.

B U R R A R D

tunnel

I N L E T

Pipeline Rd

Beaver Lake

EMPRESS OF JAPAN
GIRL IN WETSUIT (statue)

Brockton Point

TRAIN
LOOP

Tisdall

Kinglet

VANCOUVER
AQUARIUM

Way

LIGHTHOUSE

P

Mallard

Park Dr

ROSE GARDEN

Avison

Brockton Oval

TOTEM POLES

LORD STANLEY
(statue)

BROCKTON OVAL

NINE O'CLOCK GUN

? P

P

P

P

VANCOUVER
ROWING CLUB

?

nnel

C O A L

Deadman Island

P

H A R B O U R

W Georgia St

NING ROOM

START & FINISH

7 **False Creek Seawall** 10.8 km

STATS: 14 m, Year-round, TH (English Bay Park): 10 U 489614 5459454, TH (Kits Beach): 10 U 488051 5457886

This paved path snakes around the False Creek waterfront from English Bay Park in downtown's West End to Kitsilano Beach on the south side of English Bay. This picturesque route is uninterrupted, traffic free and provides exceptional views. It is immensely popular with walkers, runners and cyclists, and is a great way to get around town and check out some local landmarks. The run is described from east to west, but there are many access points along the seawall allowing you to run varying distances in either direction. The major roads providing access to False Creek are Quebec Street, West 2nd Avenue and Pacific Boulevard.

Access: *Drop a car at Kitsilano Beach before heading to the start of the run at English Bay Park.*

To Get There: *To make your car drop from downtown, start on West Georgia Street (Route 99/1A) and head west on Burrard Street. Cross the Burrard Street Bridge and veer RIGHT onto Cornwall Avenue. Continue six blocks to Yew Street, turn RIGHT and park a car at Kitsilano Beach.*

To get to the start of the run from Kitsilano Beach, head east along Cornwall Avenue and cross over the Burrard Street Bridge. Exit RIGHT onto Pacific Boulevard then immediately turn RIGHT onto Hornby Street. Turn RIGHT onto Beach Avenue and head north along the waterfront for nine blocks to English Bay Park, which is at the intersection with Denman Street.

Map: *Pages 70–71*

Fun Fact: For a small fee, the little Aquabus Water Taxi darts around False Creek transporting weary runners from one espresso stand to the next. You can hop aboard at one of several miniports (see map). Check www.theaquabus.com for a schedule and route information, or call (604) 689-5858.

The Dirt

▶ Once at English Bay Park, head toward the beachfront and locate the obvious, paved pathway. Turn LEFT (south) and jockey for position amongst the rollerbladers.

▶ Follow the waterfront path past numerous apartment buildings and various landmarks, such as BC Place Stadium, Science World, Olympic Village, Granville Island and the Planetarium. Along the way, you'll pass underneath the Burrard, Granville and Cambie Street bridges.

▶ Just west of Vanier Park (with the Planetarium) is Kitsilano Beach. Finish here, get a beer.

False Creek Seawall *Clockwise from left: Vanier Park offers spectacular views of the ocean and downtown Vancouver; the iconic Science World globe; Granville Street bridge and False Creek as seen from the Burrard Street bridge.*

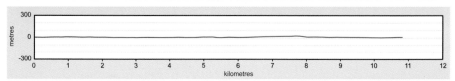

N

1 km = 5.9 cm

■ AQUABUS DOCK
---- AQUABUS ROUTE

START

ENGLISH BAY PARK

English Bay Beach

inukshuk

WEST END

Denman St.

Davie St.

Sunset Beach

Elsje Point

VANIER PARK

Pacific St.

Kitsilano Point

HR MACMILLAN
SPACE CENTRE
(PLANETARIUM)

Kitsilano Beach

P

P

Beach Ave.

BURRARD ST
BRIDGE

FINISH

Brokers Bay

P

Yew St

Cornwall Ave

7

FALSE CREEK SEAWALL

GRANVILLE
BRIDGE

W 2nd Ave

W 4th Ave

Burrard St

Granville St

99
B.C.

KITSILANO

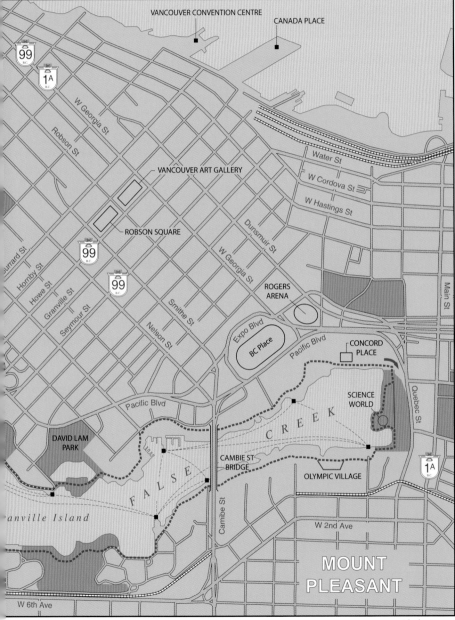

● 8 Tour de Seawall 21.8 km

STATS: 35 m, Year-round, TH: 10 U 491391 5459632

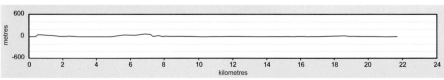

Running the entire seawall from Coal Harbour to Kits Beach makes one of the finest urban-waterfront runs in the west! Stanley Park provides your green fix and False Creek gives you the urban dose. I've described it here as a one-way half-marathon, moving from east to west.

The Dirt

▶ Once at Coal Harbour, head to the waterfront and locate the obvious pedestrian path just west of the Vancouver Convention Centre/Canada Place. Turn LEFT and run west past Coal Harbour to the marina.

▶ Stay to the RIGHT and run around the entire Stanley Park Seawall to Second Beach (see Stanley Park Seawall description).

▶ From Second Beach, keep RIGHT and continue along the waterfront to English Bay Park. From here, follow the False Creek Seawall all the way to Kitsilano Beach (see False Creek Seawall description).

Access: Drop a car at Kitsilano Beach before heading to the start of the run at Coal Harbour.

To Get There: To make your car drop from downtown, start on West Georgia Street (Route 99/1A) and head west on Burrard Street. Cross the Burrard Street Bridge and veer RIGHT onto Cornwall Avenue. Continue six blocks to Yew Street, turn RIGHT and park a car at Kits Beach.

To get to the start of the run from Kits Beach, head east along Cornwall Avenue and cross over the Burrard Street Bridge. Continue straight along Burrard Street and turn LEFT on West Georgia Street. Drive two blocks, turn RIGHT on Bute Street and drive three more blocks to the Coal Harbour area and park.

Map: Page 73

Tour de Seawall *Sunset Beach from the Burrard Street Bridge. Stanley Park is in the background.*

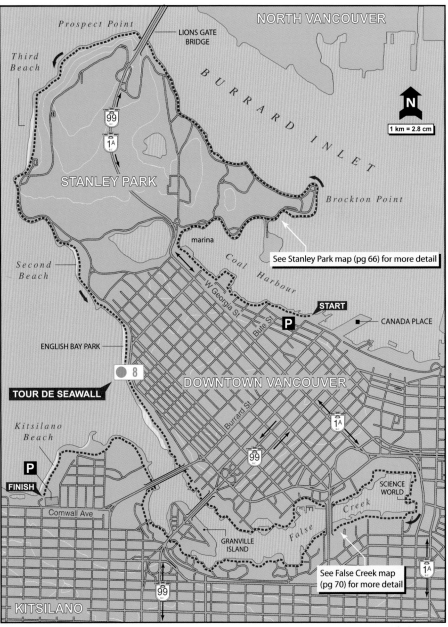

Prospect Point

NORTH VANCOUVER

LIONS GATE BRIDGE

Third Beach

BURRARD INLET

N

1 km = 2.8 cm

99

1A

STANLEY PARK

Brockton Point

marina

Coal Harbour

See Stanley Park map (pg 66) for more detail

Second Beach

W Georgia St

START

Bute St

P

CANADA PLACE

ENGLISH BAY PARK

8

DOWNTOWN VANCOUVER

TOUR DE SEAWALL

1A

Kitsilano Beach

Burrard St

99

P

SCIENCE WORLD

FINISH

Creek

Cornwall Ave

GRANVILLE ISLAND

False

1A

99

See False Creek map (pg 70) for more detail

KITSILANO

The North Shore *Charging along TNT trail on Mount Seymour.*

CHAPTER 2:

THE NORTH SHORE

Vancouver's legendary North Shore Mountains are a rugged collection of alpine peaks and densely forested hillsides that dominate the north side of Burrard Inlet. Sweeping across the lower flanks of these mountains are the communities of West Vancouver and North Vancouver, which stretch from Horseshoe Bay in the west to Deep Cove in the east. Several prominent peaks dominate the skyline, including the ski resorts of Cypress Bowl, Grouse Mountain and Mount Seymour. Lower down, the Capilano River, Lynn Creek and Seymour River are the major drainages that help define the landscape.

The North Shore is world-famous for steep, rocky and rooty terrain, and is a true haven for rainforest enthusiasts. It features the largest network of trails in the area and provides incredible opportunities for folks seeking technical objectives. Runners will discover a world of adventure as they explore this enchanting landscape.

NORTH SHORE TRAIL RUNNING ZONES

1 **Lighthouse Park**

Lighthouse Park sits on a small coastal headland in West Vancouver with over 13 kilometres of moderately challenging trails. Runners will enjoy exploring the dense, old-growth forest, secluded coves and rocky shorelines that slope gradually into the glistening ocean. Along with the iconic Point Atkinson Lighthouse and breathtaking views across Georgia Strait, Lighthouse Park makes a fine destination for short, technical runs.

2 **Nelson Canyon and Gleneagles Trails**

The Gleneagles neighbourhood near Horseshoe Bay provides access to several plumb trails worth a sniff. Nelson Canyon Park sits just above Highway 99 on the lower slopes of Black Mountain. This vibrant rainforest showcases a hidden gem, the *Whyte Lake Trail*. Just below Highway 99 is the much easier *Seaview Walk*, which gives fine views across Eagle Harbour and Georgia Strait. *Seaview Walk* easily connects with Nelson Canyon and together support a short stretch of the *Trans-Canada Trail*.

3 **Cypress Provincial Park and Hollyburn Mountain**

Cypress Provincial Park encompasses almost 3,000 hectares of backcountry terrain in West Vancouver and provides a wilderness experience within an hour of downtown Vancouver. Visitors cherish the magnificent views of Georgia Strait, Vancouver Island and the entire city of Vancouver far below. In winter, Cypress Bowl (site of the 2010 Olympics) and Hollyburn Mountain provide some of the best snow sport terrain on the North Shore. Runners can expect a remote rainforest and alpine environment with route-finding challenges.

Hollyburn Mountain sits just southeast of Cypress Bowl and offers a web of trails accessible from both the Cypress Bowl Road and the upscale residential British Properties above Highway 99. There is a healthy collection of cabins sprawled around Hollyburn and as a result there's a maze of unmapped paths. As you tour Hollyburn you'll pass some gigantic trees and many rusting relics from early century logging.

4 **Ambleside and Dundarave**

Located along the waterfront in West Vancouver are the villages of Ambleside and Dundarave, which form the primary commercial areas in the city. Marine Drive is the activity hub and is packed with boutiques, restaurants and trendy cafés. Connecting these neighbourhoods is the beloved West Vancouver Centennial Seawalk, an eight-kilometre beachfront path that is immensely popular with runners and pedestrians.

5 Capilano River Regional Park

Capilano River Regional Park contains nearly 30 kilometres of short, hilly trails lining both sides of the Capilano River. The park is characterized by west coast rainforest surrounding an impressive cliff-lined canyon full of turbulent rapids and deep, green pools. Major attractions such as Cleveland Dam, Capilano Suspension Bridge and the Capilano Fish Hatchery draw visitors from around the globe. The park makes a highly enjoyable running destination with great potential for short to moderate length variations.

6 Grouse Mountain and Mount Fromme

Just 15 minutes from downtown Vancouver, Grouse Mountain dominates the skyline directly above the Lions Gate Bridge and is easily identifiable by several unique icons: the world-famous Skyride Gondola, a giant wind turbine and an obvious ski run (the Cut) that cuts a wide path down the south face. The Grouse Chalet gives outrageous views of the city and provides convenient access to rugged backcountry. The resort welcomes countless visitors to its alpine wonderland year-round. At Grouse Mountain, your VISA card is always welcome!

Mount Fromme is Grouse's little brother to the east. With zero commercial appeal, it's often overlooked and thus sports a completely different vibe. In recent years Grouse has become the domain of the new-school tourist trekker, while Fromme appeals more to hard-core mountain bikers and granola-nibbling hippies. Geographically, the only thing separating the two is the somewhat mysterious and inhospitable Mosquito Creek. The *Baden-Powell Trail* and Old Mountain Highway provide direct access to the Fromme trails and are your reference arteries should you find yourself exploring.

The North Shore *This page: Cathy Jensen sprints up Cabin Trail on Black Mountain. Next page (counterclockwise from top left): West Vancouver Centennial Seawalk totem pole at Ambleside beach; Whyte Lake Trail in Nelson Canyon; Lion's Gate Bridge at sunset as seen from the Capilano Pacific Trail; Cypress Falls in West Vancouver.*

www.richwheater.com

7 Lynn Valley

The residential neighbourhood of Lynn Valley sits immediately northeast of Highway 1 in North Vancouver. It provides instant access to the trails of Mount Fromme, Lynn Headwaters, Lynn Canyon, Lower Seymour Conservation Reserve (LSCR) and Mount Seymour.

Lynn Headwaters Regional Park occupies nearly 5,000 hectares of wilderness rainforest in between Fromme and Seymour, and is a superb running destination. The ever-popular *Lynn Loop* is a common objective and can be incorporated into many variations ranging from 30 minutes to over six hours. Lynn Creek is the central attraction and the forested slopes surrounding it are full of steep streams, gullies, canyons and cliffs.

Lynn Canyon Park sits immediately south of Lynn Headwaters and is perhaps best known for its 50-metre-high suspension bridge. This 250-hectare municipal park showcases the treacherous Lynn Canyon, several waterfalls and some prime swimming holes. An engaging section of the *Baden-Powell Trail* runs through the entire park and several trails connect easily with neighbouring Lynn Headwaters and the LSCR.

8 Lower Seymour Conservation Reserve and Mount Seymour Provincial Park

Immediately east of Lynn Headwaters is the LSCR, a 5,600-hectare area encompassing the heavily-forested Seymour River just north of the Second Narrows bridge. Over 40 kilometres of trails lead past relics from logging, mining, fishing and farming activity in the early 1900s. Originally known as the Seymour Demonstration Forest, the LSCR provides educational programs and interpretive signs demonstrating how active management of natural resources can be sustainable.

Mount Seymour Provincial Park borders the LSCR to the east and overlooks the secluded hamlet of Deep Cove and the large inlet of Indian Arm. Seymour boasts an awesome network of lower-mountain trails frequented by both runners and mountain bikers. The alpine provides access to rugged park trails surrounding Vancouver's smallest and only family-operated ski resort.

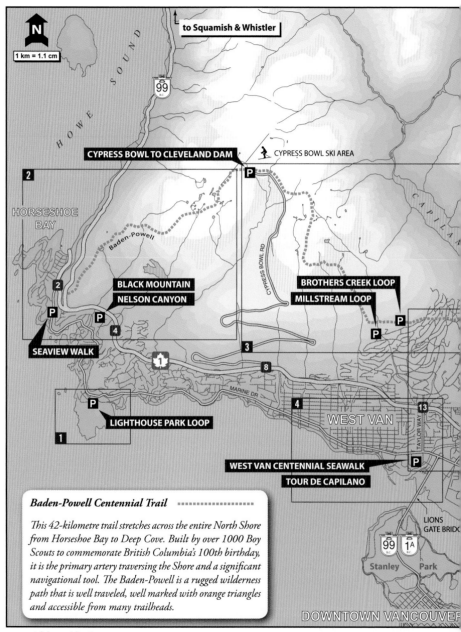

N

1 km = 1.1 cm

to Squamish & Whistler

99
B.C.

HOWE SOUND

CYPRESS BOWL TO CLEVELAND DAM

CYPRESS BOWL SKI AREA

P

CAPILAN

2

HORSESHOE BAY

Baden-Powell

2

P

P

4

SEAVIEW WALK

BLACK MOUNTAIN
NELSON CANYON

BROTHERS CREEK LOOP
MILLSTREAM LOOP

CYPRESS BOWL RD

P

P

3

8

1

P

LIGHTHOUSE PARK LOOP

MARINE DR

4

WEST VAN

13

TAYLOR WAY

P

1

WEST VAN CENTENNIAL SEAWALK

TOUR DE CAPILANO

LIONS
GATE BRIDG

99
B.C.

1A
B.C.

Stanley   Park

DOWNTOWN VANCOUVER

Baden-Powell Centennial Trail

*This 42-kilometre trail stretches across the entire North Shore
from Horseshoe Bay to Deep Cove. Built by over 1000 Boy
Scouts to commemorate British Columbia's 100th birthday,
it is the primary artery traversing the Shore and a significant
navigational tool. The Baden-Powell is a rugged wilderness
path that is well traveled, well marked with orange triangles
and accessible from many trailheads.*

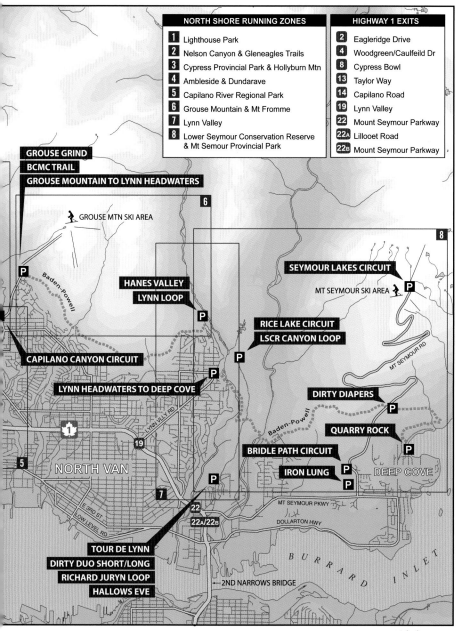

NORTH SHORE RUNNING ZONES

1. Lighthouse Park
2. Nelson Canyon & Gleneagles Trails
3. Cypress Provincial Park & Hollyburn Mtn
4. Ambleside & Dundarave
5. Capilano River Regional Park
6. Grouse Mountain & Mt Fromme
7. Lynn Valley
8. Lower Seymour Conservation Reserve & Mt Semour Provincial Park

HIGHWAY 1 EXITS

2. Eagleridge Drive
4. Woodgreen/Caulfeild Dr
8. Cypress Bowl
13. Taylor Way
14. Capilano Road
19. Lynn Valley
22. Mount Seymour Parkway
22A. Lillooet Road
22B. Mount Seymour Parkway

GROUSE GRIND
BCMC TRAIL
GROUSE MOUNTAIN TO LYNN HEADWATERS

GROUSE MTN SKI AREA

6

Baden-Powell

SEYMOUR LAKES CIRCUIT

MT SEYMOUR SKI AREA

8

HANES VALLEY
LYNN LOOP

RICE LAKE CIRCUIT
LSCR CANYON LOOP

MT SEYMOUR RD

CAPILANO CANYON CIRCUIT

LYNN HEADWATERS TO DEEP COVE

LYNN VLLY RD

DIRTY DIAPERS

Baden-Powell

QUARRY ROCK

BRIDLE PATH CIRCUIT

IRON LUNG

DEEP COVE

19

NORTH VAN

5

7

E 3RD ST
LOW LEVEL RD

22
22A/22B

MT SEYMOUR PKWY
DOLLARTON HWY

TOUR DE LYNN
DIRTY DUO SHORT/LONG
RICHARD JURYN LOOP
HALLOWS EVE

← 2ND NARROWS BRIDGE

B U R R A R D   I N L E T

■ 9 Lighthouse Park Loop ♥

3.9 km

STATS: 115 m, Year-round, TH: 10 U 480915 5464947

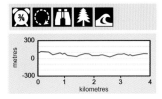

Lighthouse Park is famous for its rugged coastline, ocean views, unique arbutus trees and historic Point Atkinson lighthouse. Expect technical singletrack lined with ferns, salal and massive trees. Notice how God-beams sneak through the evergreen boughs… Om.

The Dirt

▶ From the parking lot, head through the grey gate and run south down *Beacon Lane*, the obvious wide path that leads to the lighthouse. Immediately turn LEFT onto *Salal Loop* (sign) and run uphill to a fire hydrant and a large yellow sign.

▶ Turn RIGHT and follow *Salal Loop* to a junction with *Arbutus* (sign). Turn RIGHT and run downhill to a fork (sign) and go LEFT down *Deer Fern*.

▶ Keep left past an unmarked fork and when you reach an exit trail to houses (sign), make a hard RIGHT onto the unmarked *Maple* trail. Run to a large silver rescue cache and turn LEFT onto *Arbutus* (sign).

▶ Follow *Arbutus* downhill to a wooden bench and rock step, and continue past a short access trail to Eagle Point (sign) to a junction with *Valley of the Giants* (sign). Stay LEFT along *Arbutus* to a junction with *Valley Trail* (sign). Go LEFT downhill and continue past a short access trail to Starboat Cove. ▶▶

Access: Start at the Lighthouse Park parking lot.

To Get There: If coming from downtown Vancouver, follow Route 99/1A (West Georgia Street) north over the Lions Gate Bridge and exit LEFT into West Vancouver. Reset your odometer at the Taylor Way traffic lights and head west along Marine Drive for exactly 10 km to Beacon Lane. Turn LEFT and drive 200 m to the Lighthouse Park entrance.

If coming from Highway 1 on the North Shore, take Exit 13 for Taylor Way and head downhill to Marine Drive. Turn RIGHT and drive 10 km to Beacon Lane. Turn LEFT and drive 200 m to the Lighthouse Park entrance.

Map: Pages 84–85

Lighthouse Park Loop *Clockwise from left: Point Atkinson Lighthouse as seen from West Beach; famous sign at park entrance on Marine Drive; Senja Palonen on the Shore Pine Trail; Running amongst the Arbutus trees.*

▶ Pass viewpoints on the left to reach a major intersection with *Beacon Lane* (garbage can and sign). Continue STRAIGHT (and slightly left) across the clearing, past log buildings, to *Shore Pine*.

▶ Follow *Shore Pine* past a lighthouse viewpoint and keep LEFT at a junction with *Seven Sisters* (sign). Continue toward Shore Pine Point, passing a short access trail to West Beach.

▶ At the access trail to Shore Pine Point, head RIGHT into the forest and run to a junction with *Seven Sisters* (sign). Turn LEFT and run up *Seven Sisters* to a junction that has a water spigot.

▶ At the spigot, turn LEFT onto *Juniper Loop/ Juniper Point Trail*. Keep LEFT past the first *Juniper Loop* turnoff and descend a rocky trail toward Juniper Point.

▶ Just before you get to Juniper Point, turn RIGHT onto *Juniper Loop* (sign) and go up a deluxe boardwalk and staircase to a viewing platform.

▶ Continue along *Juniper Loop* to three-way junction (sign) and go LEFT for several minutes to return to the parking lot.

Interesting Fact: Lighthouse Park houses the city's last stand of first-growth Douglas fir trees, as well as some monstrous Western hemlock and Western redcedar. Some are 200 feet tall and over 500 years old. More unique to the park is the Pacific Madrone (a.k.a. Arbutus tree), which only grows on the west coast of North America and has a distinct orange bark that peels to reveal a smooth shiny finish. Native Americans used the seasonal berries to make cider

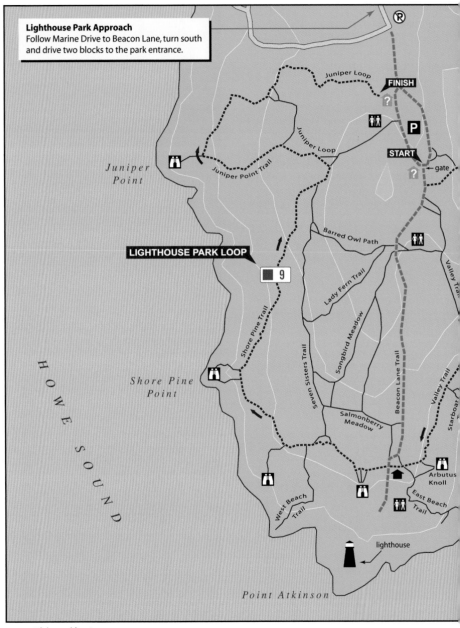

Lighthouse Park Approach
Follow Marine Drive to Beacon Lane, turn south
and drive two blocks to the park entrance.

Juniper Loop

FINISH

START

gate

Juniper Point

Juniper Point Trail

Juniper Loop

Barred Owl Path

LIGHTHOUSE PARK LOOP

■ 9

Lady Fern Trail

Shore Pine Trail

Songbird Meadow

Seven Sisters Trail

Beacon Lane Trail

Valley Trail

Valley Trail

Starboat Trail

Shore Pine Point

H O W E   S O U N D

Salmonberry Meadow

Arbutus Knoll

West Beach Trail

East Beach Trail

lighthouse

Point Atkinson

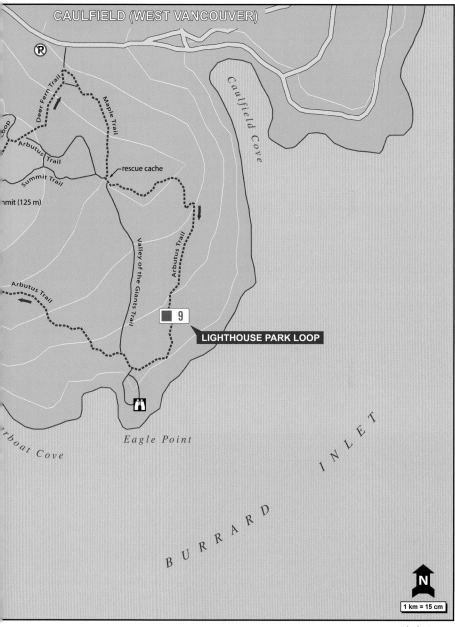

CAULFIELD (WEST VANCOUVER)

®

Deer Fern Trail

Maple Trail

Loop

Arbutus Trail

Summit Trail

rescue cache

Summit (125 m)

Valley of the Giants Trail

Arbutus Trail

Arbutus Trail

Caulfield Cove

9

LIGHTHOUSE PARK LOOP

rboat Cove

Eagle Point

BURRARD INLET

N

1 km = 15 cm

⬤ 10 Seaview Walk   3.8 km

STATS: 21 m, Year-round, TH: 10 U 479855 5467655

Located just south of Horseshoe Bay, this mellow path contours a scenic bench from Eagleridge Drive to Nelson Canyon. The wide gravel trail is flat as a crepe, super popular with dog walkers and boasts fantastic views over Eagle Harbour and Georgia Strait. It's a perfect outing for folks craving a first date with Mother Nature.

The Dirt

▶ From the parking area, head up and RIGHT onto the obvious, wide path. Cruise past mileage posts for 2 km to a junction with the *Trans-Canada Trail* (sign). Stay RIGHT and continue slightly downhill over Nelson Creek to Cranley Drive. Turn around and reverse your route to the parking area.

Variation: Want to add some technical running to your day? Try connecting the *Seaview Walk* to the gorgeous *Whyte Lake Trail* (page 88). To do so, run to the *Trans-Canada Trail* junction at the east end of the *Seaview Walk* and head uphill under the daunting highway bridge to a paved road. Turn RIGHT and cross a bridge to reach a large black water tank and a *Trans-Canada Trail* signpost. From here, follow the directions for the Nelson Canyon run (starting from the first water tank in that description). The total run length is 10 km, the difficulty is intermediate and the character is moderately strenuous.

Access: Start at a small gravel parking area on the southeast corner of Marine and Eagleridge drives in West Vancouver.

To Get There: Follow Route 99/1A (West Georgia Street) north over the Lions Gate Bridge and go LEFT into West Vancouver. At the Taylor Way traffic lights turn RIGHT and head uphill to Highway 1 and zero your odometer. Go LEFT onto Highway 1 and head west for 10.5 km to Exit 2 for Eagleridge Drive. Descend Eagleridge Drive to Marine Drive, turn LEFT and immediately LEFT again into the parking area.

Map: Pages 92–93

Seaview Walk *From left: Underneath the Highway 1/99 bridge; Eagle Harbour Yacht Club as seen from the highway. The trail traverses the top of the obvious rock bench above the yacht club.*

STATS: 172 m, Year-round, TH: 10 U 48126 5467599

This short mission leads through the lush and exotic Nelson Canyon for 2.5 kilometres to the quaint Whyte Lake. Many enjoy a refreshing dunk in the cool water before making the return journey. This is one of the most beautiful trails on the North Shore – the trees are literally covered in green fur. Listen closely for owls and watch out for Ewoks.

The Dirt

▶ From the parking lot, run past the yellow gate and go under the freeway bridge on a gravel service road. Reach a large, black water tank and continue STRAIGHT uphill following signs for the *Trans-Canada* and *Whyte Lake* trails.

▶ Quickly reach a second water tank and continue up into the forest on the *Trans-Canada Trail*. Slog uphill for 500 m to a signed junction. Turn LEFT and follow the more technical *Whyte Lake Trail* through spectacular rainforest. Along the way, pass two short paths leading right to Whyte Lake.

▶ Continue a short distance to a three-way junction below an amazing outhouse (you'll want to visit this one!) This is your turn-around point. On the way back check out the Whyte Lake viewpoint and newly constructed dock. Pretty nice woodwork!

Access: Start at a gravel parking lot beside Highway 99, just off Westport Road in West Vancouver.

To Get There: From downtown Vancouver, follow Route 99/1A (West Georgia Street) north over the Lions Gate Bridge and go LEFT into West Vancouver. Turn RIGHT at the Taylor Way traffic lights, head uphill to Highway 1 and zero your odometer. Enter the freeway westbound and drive 8.2 km toward Horseshoe Bay.

Take Exit 4 for Woodgreen/Caulfeild Drive and immediately turn LEFT onto Westport Road. Drive 200 m to a four-way stop and continue STRAIGHT ahead. Drive for 1.5 km, pass underneath the freeway and immediately turn RIGHT into the parking area.

Map: Pages 92–93

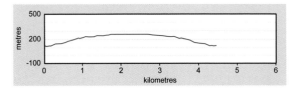

Nelson Canyon *Senja Palonen on the Whyte Lake Trail.*

Trans-Canada Trail: This country-wide route is over 20,000 km long and connects Canada's Arctic, Pacific and Atlantic coastlines! It links 400 individual trails and is rumoured to be the longest recreational route in the world. It was pieced together via a monumental volunteer effort, likely the largest ever in Canada. As you explore the North Shore trails, navigation can sometimes get confusing as you'll find *Trans-Canada Trail* markers next to existing trail markers. Just remember that the *Trans-Canada Trail* is simply a route that follows preexisting trails. For full details visit www.tctrail.ca.

▲ 12 | Black Mountain ♥♥♥   10.1 km

STATS: 1070 m, July–October, TH: 10 U 481216 5467599

This stout adventure leads through Nelson Canyon to Whyte Lake before climbing the *Baden-Powell Trail* over Black Mountain to Cypress Bowl. After a pleasant warm-up along the trail to Whyte Lake, crank up relentless switchbacks, which lead through two prominent scree slopes on the way to Eagle Bluffs – enjoy jaw-dropping views in all directions. Navigate around several small lakes before making the knee-pounding descent to Cypress Bowl. Over 1,000 m of elevation is gained in the first eight kilometres, so big lungs and bionic quads are mandatory!

The Dirt

▸ Follow the directions to Whyte Lake in the Nelson Canyon description. Run past the lake to a major trail junction with a beautiful outhouse and turn RIGHT. Contour around the lake for 200 m before trending uphill, away from the lake, on a steep and narrow section of trail. Merge with the *Baden-Powell Trail* after 300 m.

▸ Turn RIGHT and plow up the *Baden-Powell Trail*, following orange trail markers. This bit is steep and rocky, but after 600 m the trail enters thick forest and becomes soft and loamy underfoot.

▸ Continue up to a vague junction with *Donut* (tree marker). Keep RIGHT on the *Baden-Powell Trail* and tackle steep rock steps and switchbacks to the base of an exposed scree slope. Some of the sections ahead may involve minor scrambling. ▸▸

Trailhead: Shuttle a car to Cypress Bowl before heading to the start of the run at the Nelson Canyon parking lot.

To Get There: To make your car drop from downtown Vancouver, follow Route 99/1A (West Georgia Street) north over the Lions Gate Bridge and turn LEFT into West Vancouver. At the lights, turn RIGHT onto Taylor Way, drive uphill to Highway 1 and zero your odometer. Enter the freeway westbound and drive 4.5 km to Exit 8 for Cypress Bowl. Drive 15 km up Cypress Bowl Road and park a vehicle. Don't forget your keys!

To get to Nelson Canyon from Cypress Bowl, descend the road to Highway 1 and zero your odometer. Enter the freeway heading west, drive for 3.8 km and take Exit 4 for Woodgreen/Caulfeild Drive. From here, follow the Nelson Canyon directions to the gravel parking lot.

Map: Pages 92–93

Black Mountain *Clockwise from left: View of Vancouver and the Georgia Strait from Eagle Bluffs; Sam Lake, between Eagle Bluffs and Black Mountain; Catherine Jensen nearing the top of Black Mountain.*

▶ Follow cairns and flagging-tape through ankle-eating scree. Enter a short section of forest before arriving at a second scree slope. Struggle uphill for 500 m to Eagle Bluffs where you'll be rewarded with a bit of a breather. Continue up exposed rock slabs to a fantastic panorama, which includes Mount Garibaldi to the north and Vancouver and the Gulf islands to the west. It's an awesome view!

▶ Ahead, the trail climbs lightly and meanders around several alpine lakes. This section can be difficult to navigate, so pay attention and follow *only* the orange *Baden-Powell Trail* markers.

▶ Pass through a miniature swamp with a small lake on the left. Keep LEFT past two more lakes and arrive at junction with *Cabin Lake Trail* (sign). Stay RIGHT and descend a wide trail for 600 m.

▶ At the next junction, go LEFT on *Cabin Lake Trail*.

▶ After 350 m, turn RIGHT at a signpost and descend an excellent, steep and newly-constructed section of the *Baden-Powell Trail* to the Cypress Bowl downhill ski area. After you pass a ski run, descend steep switchbacks to an intersection with *Yew Lake Trail*. Turn RIGHT and run toward the ski area base.

▶ After 150 m, pass by a chairlift and follow a service road to the parking area. You're done!

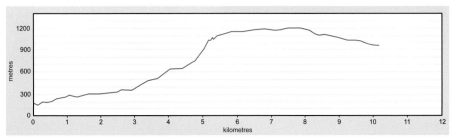

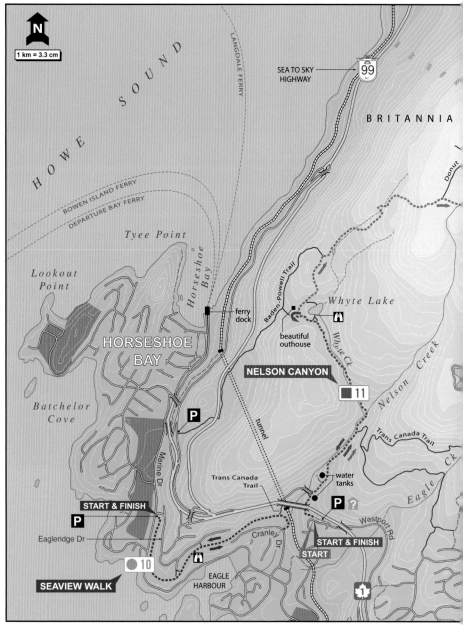

N

1 km = 3.3 cm

H O W E   S O U N D

LANGDALE FERRY

SEA TO SKY
HIGHWAY

99
B.C.

BRITANNIA

BOWEN ISLAND FERRY

DEPARTURE BAY FERRY

Tyee Point

*Lookout
Point*

Horseshoe Bay

Donut

Baden - Powell Trail

Whyte Lake

ferry
dock

beautiful
outhouse

Whyte Ck.

**HORSESHOE
BAY**

NELSON CANYON

Nelson Creek

■ **11**

*Batchelor
Cove*

tunnel

Trans Canada Trail

Eagle Ck.

water
tanks

Marine Dr

Trans Canada
Trail

P

P

?

START & FINISH

P

Eagleridge Dr

Cranley Dr

Westport Rd

START & FINISH

START

● **10**

SEAVIEW WALK

*EAGLE
HARBOUR*

1

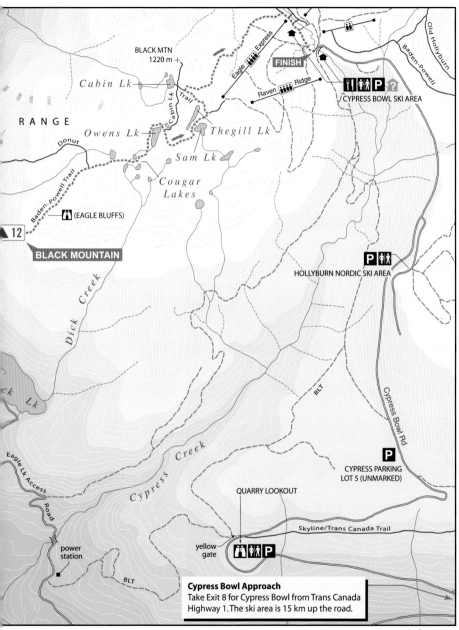

BLACK MTN
1220 m

Cabin Lk

Eagle Express

FINISH

Raven Ridge

CYPRESS BOWL SKI AREA

Old Hollyburn

Baden-Powell

R A N G E

Donut

Owens Lk

Cabin Lk Trail

Thegill Lk

Sam Lk

Cougar
Lakes

Baden-Powell Trail

12

(EAGLE BLUFFS)

BLACK MOUNTAIN

HOLLYBURN NORDIC SKI AREA

Dick Creek

Lk

BLT

Cypress Bowl Rd

Cypress Creek

CYPRESS PARKING
LOT 5 (UNMARKED)

Eagle Lk Access Road

QUARRY LOOKOUT

Skyline/Trans Canada Trail

Cypress Creek

power
station

yellow
gate

BLT

Cypress Bowl Approach
Take Exit 8 for Cypress Bowl from Trans Canada
Highway 1. The ski area is 15 km up the road.

◆ 13 Cypress
Bowl to Cleveland Dam   11.3 km

STATS: 927 m, June–November, TH: 10 U 485307 5471426

This route follows the *Baden-Powell Trail* from Cypress Bowl to Cleveland Dam. It begins with a fun traverse to Hollyburn Ridge before passing several small lakes and huts in the cross-country ski area. The trail then descends thick forest to the British Properties, where it slips through a residential neighbourhood before winding up at Cleveland Dam in Capilano River Regional Park. Hopefully your knees won't explode since this run is almost entirely downhill!

The Dirt

▶ From the ski-patrol hut and information kiosk at the top of Cypress Bowl Road, head RIGHT up a ski run for 50 m to the *Baden-Powell Trail* (sign). Enter the forest and follow the trail toward Hollyburn Ridge, passing two trails leading left up to Hollyburn Mountain. ▸▸

Access: *Shuttle a car to the Cleveland Dam before heading to the start of the run at the Cypress Bowl ski area.*

To Get There*: To make your car drop from downtown Vancouver, follow Route 99/1A (West Georgia Street) north over the Lions Gate Bridge and exit RIGHT into North Vancouver. At the first set of lights, turn LEFT and head up Capilano Road for 4 km to Cleveland Dam. Park a car.*

To get to Cypress Bowl from the Cleveland Dam, drive down Capilano Road and enter Highway 1 heading west. Drive 4.5 km and take Exit 8 for Cypress Bowl. Follow the Cypress Bowl Road all the way up the hill to the ski area.

Map: *Pages 100–101*

Cypress Bowl to Cleveland Dam
Clockwise from left: Brent Nixon crossing the power line section near the Upper Warming Hut on Hollyburn; the upper power line section on Hollyburn; typical boardwalk along the Baden-Powell Trail between Cypress Bowl and Hollyburn Nordic area; view of First Lake.

▶ Cross a small bridge then go a wee bit farther to a T-intersection and giant signpost. Turn RIGHT and follow the trail (orange markers), which meanders down Pacific ski run before dropping down past a small lake to an obvious cabin (Upper Warming Hut) on the power line.

▶ Run across the power line, pass a power tower and continue following the *Baden-Powell Trail* straight down the center of the Wells Gray ski run. Pass through an intersection with *Sitzmark* and keep LEFT past the *First Lake Trail*, which leads to Hollyburn Lodge.

▶ At the next intersection with *Sitzmark*, continue down the *Grand National* ski run following signs for the *Baden-Powell Trail*. Run past a cool little cabin (the Doghouse) to a junction with *Jack Pratt*. Go RIGHT down *Grand National* to a signpost and awesome view.

▶ Follow the loose, rocky trail down to a clearing. Stay LEFT following orange markers to a signpost marked *West Lake Trail*. Go RIGHT another 25 m to a signpost marked *Blue Gentian Lake/Baden-Powell Trail*. Enter the forest.

▶ Descend the *Baden-Powell Trail* past the *Blue Gentian Lake Trail* turn-off and then pass *Crossover* to an intersection with *Skyline* just before the power line. Turn LEFT and follow *Skyline*, which quickly merges with the *Baden-Powell Trail*.

▶ Follow the *Baden-Powell Trail* across Brother's Creek, continue downhill to the power line and merge with the Brothers Creek fire road. Continue downhill 50 m then turn LEFT back onto the *Baden-Powell Trail*. Keep descending through the residential British Properties following signs to Cleveland Dam.

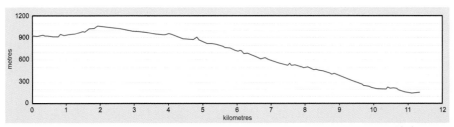

◆ 14 Millstream Loop ♡♡ 6.7 km

STATS: 303 m, April–November, TH: 10 U 488889 5466857

While this loop drags you up the strenuous *Forks* trail above Cypress Bowl's popular Highview Lookout, most of the mileage is covered traversing the *Millstream* and *Skyline* trails on lower Hollyburn Mountain. Several creek gullies are crossed amidst an old forest stuffed with Douglas fir and hemlock trees, many of which are absolutely huge! This area also houses the Lawson Creek Forestry Tour, which leads past various artifacts and mill sites from early century logging.

The Dirt

▶ From the yellow gate and signpost, head out along *Millstream* (an old road). Run past a signed junction for the *Baden-Powell Trail*, go through a chain-link fence and continue past the entrance for *Brewis* (sign).

▶ After passing a couple of streams with bridges, *Millstream* narrows and becomes a singletrack path, which leads to a ravine. Cross the ravine and continue past two vague mountain bike descents. Go through another chain-link fence to gain the Cypress Bowl Road.

▶ Turn RIGHT onto a narrow trail that climbs up a grassy bench above the road. Go through a third chain-link fence and merge LEFT onto *Forks*. Struggle up *Forks* (a popular and high-speed mountain bike descent) for 1 km to a power line.

▶ At the first signpost marked *Trans-Canada Trail*, turn RIGHT. Run the *Trans-Canada Trail* (a.k.a. *Skyline Trail*) past four major creek gullies and two junctions for *Brewis* (upper and lower). Continue along the *Trans-Canada Trail* past a fifth major creek gully.

▶ When you arrive at the *Baden-Powell Trail* intersection, turn RIGHT and descend a fire road to Millstream Road. At the bottom of the hill, turn LEFT and run back to the start.

Access: Start at the intersection of Eyremount Drive and Millstream Road in West Vancouver.

To Get There: From Highway 1 in West Vancouver, take Exit 13 for Taylor Way and zero your odometer. Head up Taylor Way to a large roundabout and turn LEFT on Southborough Drive. After 0.7 km, turn LEFT on Highland Drive. At 2.3 km, turn LEFT on Eyremount Drive. At 3 km, turn RIGHT on Millstream Road. The trailhead is immediately on your LEFT.

Map: Pages 100–101

Millstream Loop *Brent Nixon (and Daisy the dog) crossing a rickety bridge.*

Variation: A major link-up (The Hollyburn Hobble) runs Millstream Loop in its entirety, heads up Millstream Road and then tackles the full Brothers Creek Loop! This run is 16 km long, is advanced-expert in difficulty and features some beautiful, large trees along with a waterfall to keep you engaged.

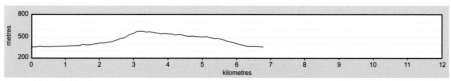

▲ 15 Brothers Creek Loop ♥♥   8.3 km

STATS: 468 m, May–November, TH: 10 U 489736 5467221

This burly little run explores the heavily-forested and highly-technical Brothers Creek drainage on lower Hollyburn Mountain. After a steady grunt up the Brothers Creek Fire Road, you'll pass some enormous trees to gain the plush Brothers Creek Bridge. From here, technical singletrack leads past mosquito-infested Lost Lake to Blue Gentian Lake before descending the west side of Brothers Creek past a gorgeous canyon and waterfall. This loop stands out as an exceptionally challenging run when wet, which it almost always is.

The Dirt

▸ From the trailhead, go through a chain-link fence and grind up *Brothers Creek Fire Road* to a power line. Run LEFT under the power line for 100 m then continue up *Brothers Creek Fire Road*, following signs for the Brothers Creek Forestry Heritage Tour.

▸▸

Access: *As for Millstream Loop, but go an additional 1 km up Millstream Road, past Henlow Road, and look for a small spur road on the left. A large gate with a Brothers Creek sign marks the trailhead.*

Map: *Pages 100–101*

Brothers Creek Loop *Clockwise from lower left: Trailhead signpost; Kristina Jenei near Lost Lake; Brent Nixon near Lost Lake; relic from the neglected forestry tour; Kristina Jenei amongst massive Western Hemlock and Douglas firs.*

▶ After 200 m on the road, reach a junction with *Balantree* and keep LEFT. After 500 m, reach a junction with *Crossover* (look for the picnic table) and keep RIGHT. Continue up *Brothers Creek Fire Road*, which gradually levels off.

▶ When you reach a large bridge over Brothers Creek (3 km to here), turn RIGHT and climb a technical trail to Lost Lake.

▶ At Lost Lake, turn LEFT and continue toward Blue Gentian Lake (watch for tuna-tin trail markers). En route, you'll pass a large sign near cliffs marked "Closed Area" before rock-hopping across Brothers Creek (no bridge). Just past the creek is a junction with the *West Lake Trail* (sign). Keep LEFT for another 25 m and reach a boardwalk at Blue Gentian Lake.

▶ Stay LEFT along the lakeshore for 100 m then descend the trail back to a large bridge over Brothers Creek. Do NOT cross the bridge, but stay RIGHT and descend the *Brothers Creek Trail* to a junction with *Crossover*.

▶ Keep LEFT for a few paces then go LEFT onto *Crossover* and down to another bridge spanning Brothers Creek. Cross the bridge and continue on *Crossover* straight across an old road cut (easy to miss) and descend back to the *Brothers Creek Fire Road* (at the picnic table).

▶ Turn RIGHT down *Brothers Creek Fire Road* to a junction with *Balantree*. Keep RIGHT and descend to a power line. Veer LEFT under the power line for 100 m then deke RIGHT down the fire road back to the trailhead and your cookies.

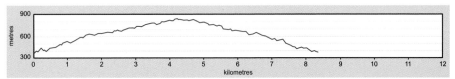

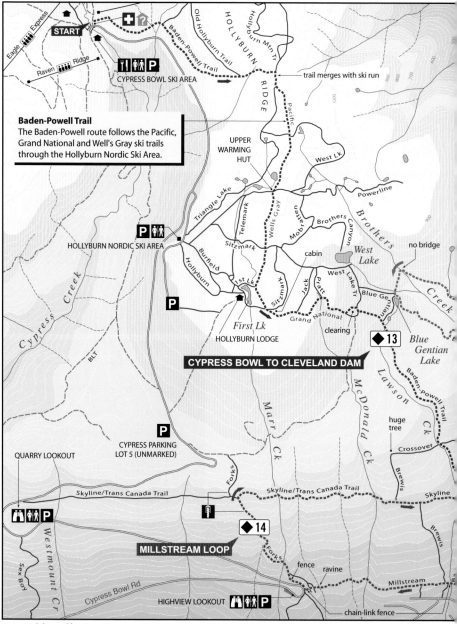

Baden-Powell Trail
The Baden-Powell route follows the Pacific, Grand National and Well's Gray ski trails through the Hollyburn Nordic Ski Area.

START

Eagle Express

Raven Ridge

CYPRESS BOWL SKI AREA

HOLLYBURN RIDGE

Old Hollyburn Trail

Baden-Powell Trail

Hollyburn Mtn Tr

Pacific

trail merges with ski run

UPPER WARMING HUT

West Lk.

Powerline

Triangle Lake

Telemark

Wells Gray

Mobratten

Brothers

Canyon

Brothers

West Lake

no bridge

HOLLYBURN NORDIC SKI AREA

Burfield

Sitzmark

cabin

West Lake Tr

Hollyburn

1st Lk

Sitzmark

Jack

Pratt

Blue Ge..

Creek

First Lk

Grand National

clearing

◆ 13

Blue Gentian Lake

HOLLYBURN LODGE

CYPRESS BOWL TO CLEVELAND DAM

Cypress Creek

BLT

Marr Ck

McDonald Ck

Lawson

Ck

huge tree

Crossover

Brewis

CYPRESS PARKING LOT 5 (UNMARKED)

QUARRY LOOKOUT

Skyline/Trans Canada Trail

Forks

Skyline/Trans Canada Trail

Skyline

Westmount Cr

Sex Boy

◆ 14

MILLSTREAM LOOP

Forks

fence

ravine

Brewis

Millstream

Cypress Bowl Rd

HIGHVIEW LOOKOUT

chain-link fence

www.quickdrawpublications.com

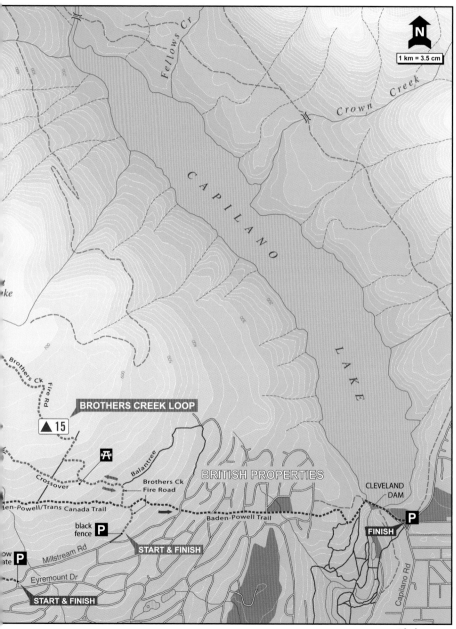

CAPILANO LAKE

Fellows Cr

Crown Creek

Brothers Ck Fire Rd

BROTHERS CREEK LOOP

▲15

Balantree

Crossover

Brothers Ck Fire Road

BRITISH PROPERTIES

CLEVELAND DAM

Baden-Powell/Trans Canada Trail

Baden-Powell Trail

black fence

FINISH

START & FINISH

Millstream Rd

Eyremount Dr

START & FINISH

Capilano Rd

1 km = 3.5 cm

16 West
Vancouver Centennial Seawalk   8.6 km
STATS: 18 m, Year-round, TH: 10 U 490233 5463544

This is the charming seaside promenade that stretches for eight kilometres between Park Royal Shopping Center and Dundarave Beach Park. The Seawalk is deservedly popular as it's completely flat and gives perfect views of Burrard Inlet and English Bay. It's easily accessible from anywhere along the Ambleside to Dundarave waterfront, so you can run any distance you choose in either direction. I've described the entire path from east to west.

The Dirt

▶ From the parking area, look for the paved pedestrian path near the Capilano River. Turn RIGHT and start running.

▶ Head through a short, forested stretch to reach a train bridge and Ambleside Dog Park. Keep LEFT through the dog area and continue past a golf course and a duck pond to the beachfront.

▶ Continue past Ambleside Beach to 13th Street. Stay LEFT and follow Argyle Avenue past the Hollyburn Sailing Club, Ferry Building Art Gallery and John Lawson Park (picnic area).

▶ Keep LEFT toward the waterfront and follow the seaside path to Dundarave Beach Park. Turn around and retrace your steps back to the Park Royal Shopping Centre.

Variations: To reduce the distance, try one of these options: Park Royal Shopping Centre to John Lawson Park and back (5 km), Ambleside Park train bridge to John Lawson Park and back (4 km), Dundarave Beach Park to Hollyburn Sailing Club at 13th Street and back (6 km), or Dundarave Beach Park to Ambleside Park train bridge and back (10 km).

Access: Start at the bottom of Taylor Way, around the back of the south side of the Park Royal Shopping Center.

To Get There: From downtown Vancouver, follow Route 99/1A (West Georgia Street) north over the Lions Gate Bridge and exit LEFT into West Vancouver. Turn LEFT at the Taylor Way traffic lights and head down and around the back (south) side of the Park Royal Shopping Centre and park.

Map: Pages 104–105

West Vancouver Centennial Seawalk *Clockwise from below: Ferry Building Art Gallery; Ambleside Beach; waves spray the Dundarave seawall.*

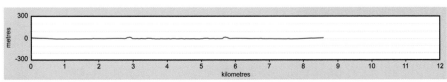

DUNDARAVE

Marine Dr

21st St

DUNDARAVE PIER

DUNDARAVE BEACH PARK

WEST VANCOUVER CENTENNIAL SEAWALK

16

Argyle Ave

P

JOHN LAWSON PARK

Navvy Jack Point

run along Argyle
Ave for 5 blocks

P (along Argyle Av

B U R R A R D

I N L E T

N

1 km = 6.0 cm

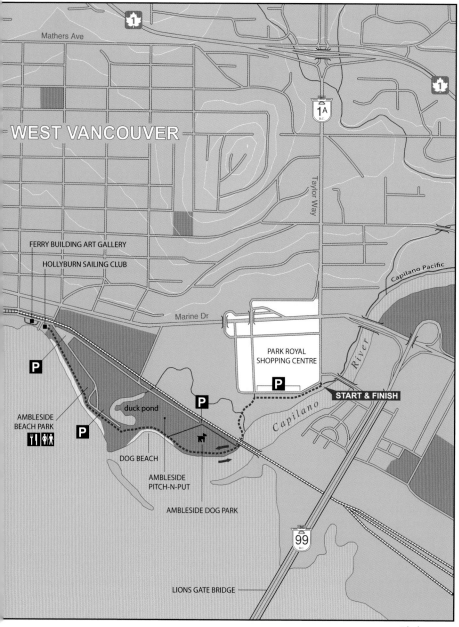

■ 17 | Tour de Capilano ♥

12.7 km

STATS: 12.7 km, 136 m, Year-round, TH: 10 U 490233 5463544

This mostly non-technical circuit explores Capilano River Regional Park and features the *Capilano Pacific* trail, which runs the full length of the river. The route has several challenging sections, one big climb and tours past an interesting fish hatchery as well as the mighty Cleveland Dam. There are several logical access points if you wish to cut or add mileage.

Access: *Start behind the Park Royal Shopping Centre in West Vancouver, same as for the West Vancouver Centennial Seawalk.*

Map: *Page 112–113*

The Dirt

▶ From the bottom of Taylor Way, pick up the wide path by the Capilano River and head north (upriver), away from the mall. Go under a bridge and continue past office buildings and condos, which are on your left. This section will feel a tad industrial.

▶ Run underneath the Marine Drive bridge and past apartment buildings to Clyde Avenue. Stay to the RIGHT and pass a seniors home on your left. Once past the buildings, turn LEFT and follow *Capilano Pacific* (sign) uphill to Keith Road.

▶ Turn RIGHT and run Keith Road for 450 m. At the end, veer LEFT and go under the large highway bridge. About 350 m past the bridge, reach a yellow gate and information kiosk, which is the entrance to Capilano River Regional Park.

▶ Continue up *Capilano Pacific,* staying RIGHT at the access trails to Moyne Drive and Rabbit Lane. The trail soon becomes technical and much more forested. Continue past a second trail to Rabbit Lane. Just ahead is an awesome viewpoint overlooking the Capilano River.

▶ Continue along *Capilano Pacific* and keep RIGHT past an unmarked junction to reach an obvious clearing. At the sign, turn RIGHT and descend *Shinglebolt* for 250 m to a service road.

▶ Turn RIGHT at the road and follow it across the Pipe Bridge. After the bridge, turn RIGHT onto *Chinook* and run a short but very technical stretch of trail uphill for 200 m.

▶ Stay to the RIGHT and descend steps, then follow rolling single-track to a sign where *Chinook* meets *Pipeline* (a gravel road). Turn LEFT and follow *Pipeline* toward the fish hatchery. ▸▸

Variation 1: Use Rabbit Lane to access *Capilano Pacific* and cut your running time in half. To get there from Highway 1 in West Vancouver, take Exit 13 for Taylor Way and head uphill to a large roundabout. Turn RIGHT on Stevens Drive and follow this past Hadden Drive. Turn RIGHT on Rabbit Lane and follow the road to a small parking pullout on the RIGHT. Take the short access trail from here to *Capilano Pacific* and run the lower section between Rabbit Lane and the Park Royal Shopping Centre for a nice, easy outing. Budget about 45 minutes for this out-and-back trip. Enjoy nice views in an urban setting that is accessible year-round.

Variation 2: Use the same approach as above, but run the upper portion of *Capilano Pacific* from Rabbit Lane to Cleveland Dam. This is far more engaging and assumes all the characteristics of the full Tour de Capilano. Budget about one hour for this 7 km loop run.

Tour de Capilano *The clean waters of the Capilano River viewed through lush undergrowth from the Coho Loop trail.*

▶ When you reach a fire hydrant, turn RIGHT and follow *Coho Loop* to the left of some cabins. Go LEFT at a sign toward the fish hatchery.

▶ Keep to the RIGHT along *Coho Loop*. Pass the Cable Pool and a large bridge before trending RIGHT through a picnic area and gazebo. Cross the road by the fish hatchery and take *Palisades* up to a large grass field at the Cleveland Dam.

▶ Head LEFT across the field, past toilets and an information kiosk. Follow the obvious paved road across the Cleveland Dam to a gravel clearing. Veer LEFT across the clearing and take the LEFT fork down *Capilano Pacific*.

▶ Pass *Shinglebolt* (on the right) and descend about 300 m to another trail fork. Turn RIGHT (away from the service road) onto *Capilano Pacific* and continue running, eventually going STRAIGHT through a large intersection with *Shinglebolt*. Follow *Capilano Pacific* all the way back to Park Royal.

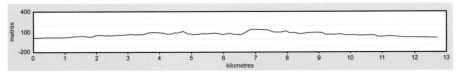

■ 18 | Capilano Canyon Circuit ♥♥   7.0 km

STATS: 120 m, March–December, TH: 10 U 492150 5467388

This little rip takes you across the scenic Cleveland Dam before diving into a tight maze of steep trails lining Capilano Canyon. Many short hills will surely get you sweatin' as you charge past cliffs, rapids, whirlpools and waterfalls amidst the refreshing rainforest.

The Dirt

▸ From the parking area, head southwest to the information kiosk and toilets. From here, turn RIGHT and follow the paved road across Cleveland Dam to a gravel clearing. Veer LEFT through the clearing to a fork. Head RIGHT up a service road toward the *Baden-Powell*, *Brothers Creek* and *Trans-Canada* trails.

▸ After 250 m, turn LEFT onto *Shinglebolt* (sign). The trail is flat at first, but suddenly drops downhill to an obvious and heavily-rooted mound on the right side. Tackle the roots to gain the top of a small knoll (sign). Turn RIGHT, run down *Shinglebolt* and, at a wooden bench, turn RIGHT (red tree markers) and continue downhill to a junction with *Capilano Pacific*.

▸ Turn LEFT on *Capilano Pacific* and run to a large intersection with two benches. Turn RIGHT down *Shinglebolt* to a service road. Cross the road and continue down to a map (DO NOT cross the Pipe Bridge). You are now on *Coho Loop*.

▸ Follow *Coho Loop* to a large bridge over the Capilano River, turn RIGHT and cross the bridge. Hang a RIGHT and follow *Coho Loop* (marked as the *Trans-Canada Trail*), avoiding all trails to the left.

▸ Pass the Cable Pool viewpoint and keep RIGHT along *Coho Loop* to an intersection with *Pipeline* (a service road). At a large sign marked "Danger Cliffs", continue STRAIGHT across and follow *Chinook* for a brief but rugged section.

▸ At an unmarked junction, keep RIGHT along *Chinook* and descend steps. At the bottom, veer left along rolling singletrack then continue uphill past a sign for the *Trans-Canada Trail*.

▸ *Chinook* soon merges with *Pipeline* (the service road). Keep RIGHT along *Chinook* to a large yellow "Caution" sign and a yellow gate at the park entrance. Turn LEFT and follow *Pipeline* for 350 m to where *Chinook* merges on the left side (sign). Get back

▸▸

Access: Start at the Cleveland Dam parking area, near the top of Capilano Road.

To Get There: If approaching from Highway 1 on the North Shore, take Exit 14 for Capilano Road. Head uphill, past the Capilano Suspension Bridge and the fish hatchery, and turn LEFT into Capilano River Regional Park's Cleveland Dam parking area (the second park entrance on the LEFT).

If coming from downtown Vancouver, follow Route 1A/99 (West Georgia Street) north across the Lions Gate Bridge. Exit RIGHT into North Vancouver and turn LEFT at the first set of traffic lights onto Capilano Road. Drive 4 km uphill to the parking area mentioned above.

Map: Page 112–113

Capilano Canyon Circuit *Strict signage warns of the dangers along Chinook (below); Senja Palonen glides past sword ferns on Capilano Pacific (right).*

Capilano Canyon Circuit *Clockwise from left: The mighty Capilano River as seen from Coho Loop; Sword Ferns blanket the slopes along Chinook; damp conditions on Coho Loop.*

onto *Chinook* and go RIGHT, downhill at first, then back up the endless steps to an unmarked junction.

▶ This time, go RIGHT and uphill for 100 m to *Pipeline* (a road with a fire hydrant). Cross the road and follow the trail leading LEFT past cabins to a sign. Turn LEFT and head toward the fish hatchery.

▶ Merge RIGHT onto *Coho Loop* and run to the bridge over the Capilano River. Cross the bridge and turn RIGHT onto *Giant Fir.*

▶ Run *Giant Fir* past an unmarked trail (on the left) and, 100 m further, reach another junction. Go STRAIGHT along the *Second Canyon Viewpoint Trail* for 150 m to an awesome viewpoint overlooking Cleveland Dam and the Capilano Hatchery. Retrace your steps 150 m, turn RIGHT and go up *Giant Fir* to a gravel service road.

▶ Turn RIGHT, run uphill for 25 m and go LEFT on *Capilano Pacific* to a large intersection with a sign and benches. Go RIGHT on *Shinglebolt* (a vague entrance) and run uphill past a wooden bench. Turn RIGHT at a sign and continue along *Shinglebolt.*

▶ After 450 m, *Shinglebolt* merges with *Capilano Pacific*. Keep LEFT and head back to the gravel clearing. Keep RIGHT through the clearing and run across the Cleveland Dam and back to the parking lot.

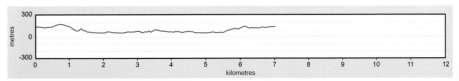

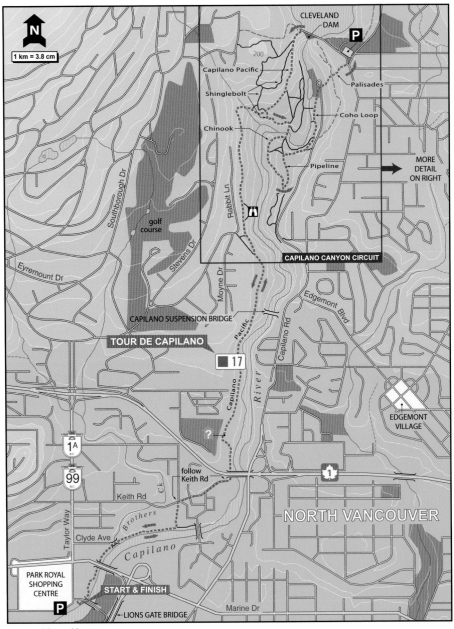

N

1 km = 3.8 cm

CLEVELAND DAM

P

200

Capilano Pacific

Palisades

Shinglebolt

Coho Loop

Chinook

Pipeline

MORE DETAIL ON RIGHT

Rabbit Ln

CAPILANO CANYON CIRCUIT

Southborough Dr

golf course

Stevens Dr

Eyremount Dr

Moyne Dr

Edgemont Blvd

CAPILANO SUSPENSION BRIDGE

Pacific

Capilano Rd

TOUR DE CAPILANO

17

Capilano

River

EDGEMONT VILLAGE

1A
B.C.

99
B.C.

?

follow Keith Rd

Keith Rd

Taylor Way

Clyde Ave

Brothers

Capilano

NORTH VANCOUVER

PARK ROYAL SHOPPING CENTRE

P

START & FINISH

← LIONS GATE BRIDGE

Marine Dr

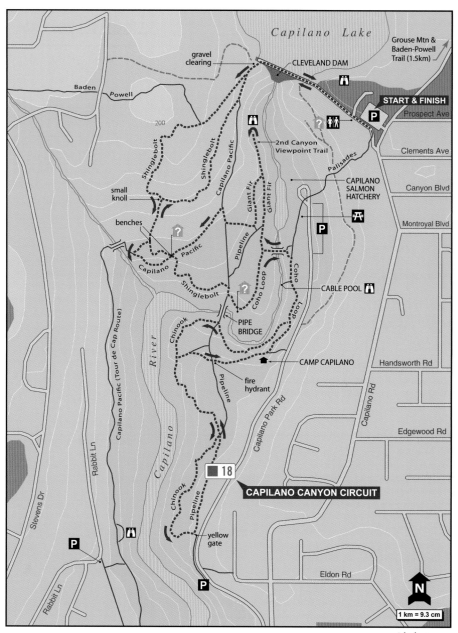

Capilano Lake

gravel clearing

CLEVELAND DAM

Grouse Mtn & Baden-Powell Trail (1.5km)

START & FINISH

P

Prospect Ave

Baden Powell

200

2nd Canyon Viewpoint Trail

?

Clements Ave

Palisades

CAPILANO SALMON HATCHERY

Canyon Blvd

Shinglebolt

Shinglebolt

Capilano Pacific

Giant Fir

Giant Fir

small knoll

P

Montroyal Blvd

benches

Capilano

Pacific

?

Pipeline

Coho Loop

Coho Loop

Shinglebolt

?

CABLE POOL

PIPE BRIDGE

Chinook

CAMP CAPILANO

Handsworth Rd

River

Pipeline

fire hydrant

Capilano Pacific (Tour de Cap Route)

Capilano Park Rd

Capilano Rd

Edgewood Rd

Capilano

Chinook

Pipeline

18

CAPILANO CANYON CIRCUIT

Rabbit Ln

Stevens Dr

P

yellow gate

Eldon Rd

P

Rabbit Ln

N

1 km = 9.3 cm

◆ 19 Grouse Grind ♥♥♥ 2.1 km

STATS: 794 m, May–November TH: 10 U 492837 5468715

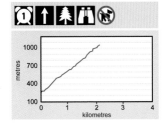

The *Grouse Grind* charges straight up an unrelenting series of steep stairs and switchbacks for almost 800 m (2640 ft), and provides a fun, powerful workout on one of the best-known trails in the country. On the way up, expect bumper-to-bumper traffic and plenty of Starbucks-toting tourists. Upon reaching the top, check out the world famous Grouse Mountain Chalet, where you can nurse a cold beer on the patio before paying $10 to descend the gondola (downhill traffic on the trail is prohibited).

The "Grind Timer Program" provides participating runners an opportunity to check their time against fellow runners on a mountaintop video screen (the current record is a blazing 23:48 minutes). If you finish in under 45 minutes you're pretty darn fit and if you're under 35 minutes you're a total rock star. Any faster than this and you should be signing autographs at the base.

Check with Grouse Mountain for official season opening times. Also note that the top of Grouse Mountain is often way cooler than the bottom. If you plan to linger up high be sure to pack a warm layer and warm hat. It gets chilly up there!

The Dirt

▸ Follow the herd to the large gate and information kiosk in the upper corner of parking lot D at the base of Grouse Mountain. Head up the trail for 200 m to a junction with the *Baden-Powell Trail* and go LEFT.

▸ Blast uphill past millions of enormous signs marked GG (*Grouse Grind)*. After 700 m, march LEFT across an obvious bridge.

▸ Continue up the steep trail passing signs that indicate the distance of your progress along the trail (¼, ½ and ¾) until you reach the open alpine. The Grouse Mountain Chalet is straight ahead.

▸ Go check out the grizzly bear pen, then storm the chalet for an espresso and a $10 gondola pass to descend the mountain (downhill traffic is prohibited on the *Grind)*.

Access: The trailhead is located at the base of Grouse Mountain in North Vancouver.

To Get There: From downtown Vancouver, follow Route 99/1A (West Georgia Street) north across the Lions Gate Bridge and exit RIGHT into North Vancouver. At the first set of lights turn LEFT on Capilano Road and drive 5.5 km uphill to the base of Grouse Mountain. Parking lot D is the first one on the right as you approach.

If coming from Highway 1 in North Vancouver, take Exit 14 for Capilano Road. Turn RIGHT and drive uphill for 4.5 km to the base of Grouse Mountain.

Map: Pages 122–123

Grouse Grind *From left: The trail follows terrain just right of the gondola; Senja Palonen topping out just below the Grouse Mountain Chalet.*

◆ 20 | BCMC Trail ♥♥♥   2.1 km

STATS: 794 m, May–November, TH: 10 U 492837 5468715

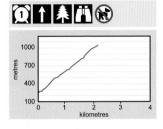

The *BCMC Trail* is the *Grouse Grind's* sober sister and tackles a similarly strenuous route directly up the mountain. Equally excellent, it receives far fewer ascents than the *Grind* and makes a fine alternative to the circus mayhem next door. The path is more natural underfoot and loaded with switchbacks and steep, incredibly jumbled root systems. It's a stout workout sure to leave your lungs and legs pleading for mercy. Finally, don't forget to bring a spare layer and warm hat. It's far cooler at the top of Grouse Mountain than the base!

Access: *Same as for the Grouse Grind.*

Map: *Pages 122–123*

The Dirt

▶ Locate parking lot D as for the *Grouse Grind* and begin at the obvious large gate and information kiosk. Head uphill for 200 m and go RIGHT at the first signpost for the *Baden-Powell Trail* (the *Grind* goes left). Approximately 25 m ahead, turn LEFT onto the well-marked *BCMC Trail* and begin cranking up steep switchbacks past many trail markers.

▶ Near the top, the trail eases off dramatically, meanders and becomes infested with roots. The path drops slightly downhill to a creek crossing before following braided exits to a wide path/service road.

▶ Stay LEFT and run toward the Grouse Chalet. Head inside for your $10 gondola pass to descend the mountain (forget the trees, save your knees).

BCMC Trail *Clockwise from bottom left: Forested terrain along the BCMC Trail; rough, but functional signage; Andrew Fodor and Josie Hetyei looking fresh despite the trail's grueling uphill challenge.*

◆ 21 Grouse Mountain to Lynn Headwaters ♥♥

7.7 km

STATS: 325 m, March–December, TH: 10 U 492837 5468715

Let's get ready to rumble! This grueling segment of the *Baden-Powell Trail* features wildly technical and hilly terrain as it traverses the lower slopes of Grouse Mountain and Mount Fromme before winding up in Lynn Valley. This exotic landscape is bursting with roots, rocks and stream crossings, and is tamed only by the occasional fantastic trail work courtesy of the North Shore Mountain Bike Association (NSMBA). Several sketchy junctions have recently sprouted fresh signage. Still, you'll need to pay close attention and follow only the orange *Baden-Powell Trail* markers. You can't claim North Shore hard-man status until you slay this dragon.

The Dirt

▸ Start at the well-marked gate and information kiosk for the *Grouse Grind* and *Baden-Powell Trail*. Run 200 m to a junction and go ▸▸

Access: The trailhead is located at the base of Grouse Mountain in North Vancouver. A car shuttle to Lynn Headwaters Park is required beforehand.

To Get There: To make your car drop from Highway 1 in North Vancouver, take Exit 19 for Lynn Valley. Follow Lynn Valley Road northeast for 3 km to a park entrance gate on the corner of Lynn Valley and Dempsey roads. Enter the park and drive 1 km along the ever-narrowing Lynn Valley Road, passing two overflow parking areas en route to the main parking area. Leave a car here.

To get to Grouse Mountain from Lynn Headwaters Park, drive down Lynn Valley Road to Highway 1 and enter the freeway heading west. Take Exit 14 for Capilano Road, turn RIGHT and drive uphill for 4.5 km to the base of Grouse Mountain. Parking lot D is the first on the right as you approach.

Map: Pages 122–123

Interesting Idea: One alternative to car shuttling is to take a taxi. If you choose to do this I suggest leaving your car at the end of your run. This way you'll have warm clothing and grub waiting at the finish line

Grouse Mountain to Lynn Headwaters *Kristina Jenei side-hilling along the base of Grouse Mountain (left) and approaching the Old Mountain Highway crossing (right).*

RIGHT along the *Baden-Powell Trail* (*Grouse Grind* goes left). Run 50 m further to a turnoff for the *BCMC Trail* and keep RIGHT, continuing along the *Baden-Powell Trail*. Initially, the track is steep and nasty, but it soon levels off giving way to lots of technical side-hill running.

▶ Keep RIGHT past a signed junction with *Larsen*, then cross a major creek gully. Continue along the *Baden-Powell Trail*, passing two unmarked paths (the *McKay Creek Trail*) that lead downhill. Just ahead, cross a second major creek gully.

▶ Keep cruising along the *Baden-Powell Trail* and stay RIGHT past a signed junction with the *Old BCMC Trail*. A little further you'll keep LEFT past a trail that exits to Skyline Drive.

▶ Descend a short switchback, exit the forest and continue to a giant signpost marked *Baden-Powell Trail*. Follow the old road, which curves around to the right, to another large signpost and turn LEFT down the *Baden-Powell Trail*. Continue down to Mosquito Creek (past a house with red roof) and across the bridge.

▶ Once across the bridge stay LEFT up the *Baden-Powell Trail* (sign) past a large water tank to a junction. Go RIGHT uphill and quickly gain another junction with *Water Tower Trail*. Go RIGHT a short distance then turn LEFT along the *Baden-Powell Trail* toward Mountain Highway (going right leads to Prospect Road and the power line). You are now traversing Mount Fromme. Follow the orange markers! ▶▶

▶ Cruise for a while to an intersection with *St. George's* (there's a nice bench here and a good view). Continue following orange *Baden-Powell Trail* markers to Mountain Highway and Lynn Valley. Many unmarked mountain bike trails cross over this stretch so be aware of riders and don't deviate onto unmarked paths!

▶ After crossing several small streams and a metal bridge over Abelard Creek, the trail drops down to Mountain Highway (a gravel road) and a water fountain. Turn LEFT then immediately turn RIGHT onto the *Baden-Powell Trail* and follow it to Lynn Headwaters. Stay LEFT past an exit to McNair Street. Run 50 m further and keep RIGHT past a signed junction (the Griffin exit) and continue past a habitat restoration project.

▶ Descend a steep twisty staircase to Lynn Valley Road. Turn LEFT and run 150 m to Lynn Headwaters parking area.

Grouse Mountain to Lynn Headwaters *Counterclockwise from below: New boardwalk on Mount Fromme courtesy of NSMBA; accommodating different user groups; Kristina Jenei tackles the gnarr on Grouse Mountain.*

Variations: This route is equally good when run in the opposite direction, so a full out-and-back run of 16 km is possible with no car shuttle required. The following out-and-back options are shorter and are also recommended: Grouse Mountain to Skyline Drive and back (5 km), Grouse Mountain to *St. George's* bench and back (8 km), Mountain Highway to *St. George's* bench and back (6 km), and Lynn Headwaters to *St. George's* bench and back (8 km).

Finally, when appropriate, consider using the power line between Grouse Mountain parking lot D and Skyline Drive as a return route instead of backtracking on the *Baden-Powell Trail*. This option is faster and easier.

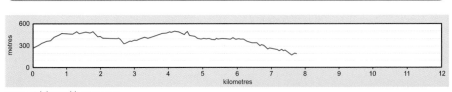

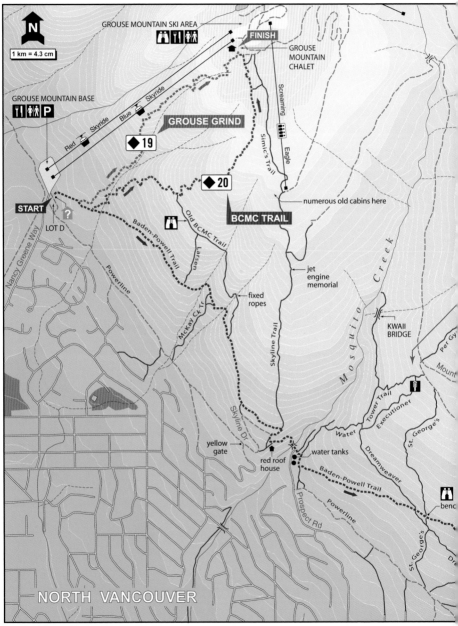

N

1 km = 4.3 cm

GROUSE MOUNTAIN SKI AREA

FINISH

GROUSE MOUNTAIN CHALET

GROUSE MOUNTAIN BASE

Red Skyride   Blue Skyride

GROUSE GRIND

◆ 19

◆ 20

Simic's Trail

Screaming Eagle

numerous old cabins here

BCMC TRAIL

START

LOT D

Nancy Greene Way

Baden-Powell Trail

Old BCMC Trail

Larsen

Powerline

McKay Ck Tr.

Skyline Trail

fixed ropes

jet engine memorial

Mosquito Creek

KWAII BRIDGE

Per Gy

Mount

Skyline Dr

yellow gate

red roof house

water tanks

Water   Tower Trail   Executioner

St. George's

Dreamweaver

Baden-Powell Trail

Prospect Rd

Powerline

St. George's

benc

Dre

NORTH VANCOUVER

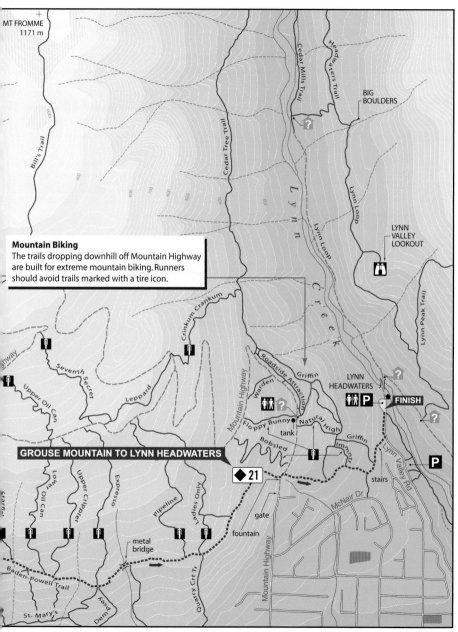

MT FROMME
1171 m

BIG
BOULDERS

Cedar Mills Trail

Headwaters Trail

Bill's Trail

Cedar Tree Trail

Lynn Loop

LYNN
VALLEY
LOOKOUT

Lynn Creek

Lynn Loop

Lynn Peak Trail

Mountain Biking
The trails dropping downhill off Mountain Highway
are built for extreme mountain biking. Runners
should avoid trails marked with a tire icon.

Crinkum Crankum

Roadside Attraction

Griffin

LYNN
HEADWATERS

FINISH

Seventh Secret

Upper Oil Can

Leppard

Warden

Mountain Highway

Floppy Bunny

Natural High

Bobsled

tank

Griffin

Imont

GROUSE MOUNTAIN TO LYNN HEADWATERS

◆ 21

stairs

Lynn Valley Rd

P

Lower Oil Can

Upper Crippler

Expresso

Pipeline

Ladies Only

gate

fountain

McNair Dr

Mountain Highway

metal
bridge

Baden-Powell Trail

Daisy Dem

Quarry Crt Tr

St. Mary's

■ 22 Lynn Loop ♥   5.6 km

STATS: 188 m, Year-round, TH: 10 U 497978 5467466

Lynn Loop is an excellent intermediate trail run and an area favourite. The first half makes a technical traverse of the forested hillside above Lynn Creek; the second half tackles steep switchbacks that bring you down to a wide gravel path that leads back to the parking area. Most of *Lynn Loop* is rolling or flat, but a couple of notable hills will surely get your ticker pumping! This description is for the standard, short *Lynn Loop*, but many variations are commonly made.

The Dirt

▶ From the parking lot, run through the picnic area and cross a bridge over Lynn Creek to reach a junction and map kiosk. Turn RIGHT and follow a gravel road for 400 m to another map and the start of *Lynn Loop*.

▶ Turn LEFT onto *Lynn Loop* and struggle up a short hill for a few minutes. The trail soon levels off and becomes much rougher as it traverses the hillside high above Lynn Creek.

▶ Keep LEFT past trails to *Lynn Peak*, *Lynn Valley Lookout* and *Big Boulders* (a point of interest). After 3.5 km, reach a junction with the *Headwaters Trail* (sign).

▶ Turn LEFT and descend switchbacks to the valley floor, then turn LEFT and follow a wide gravel path adjacent to Lynn Creek back to the parking area.

Access: Start at the main parking lot for Lynn Headwaters Regional Park.

To Get There: From Highway 1 in North Vancouver, take Exit 19 for Lynn Valley. Follow Lynn Valley Road northeast for 3 km to the park entrance on the corner of Lynn Valley and Dempsey roads. Follow the narrow park road for 1 km to its end (two overflow parking lots are passed before the main parking lot).

Note: As you approach Lynn Headwaters Park, DO NOT go down Peter's Road to the Lynn Canyon Suspension Bridge and Ecology Center. This is a common error.

Map: Page 125

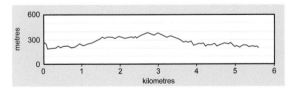

Variation: *Long Lynn Loop* is a very technical extension of the busy *Lynn Loop*. It leads from the top of the switchbacks (see *Lynn Loop* description) north along *Headwaters Trail* and over super-technical, rolling terrain to a huge clearing by the creek, the Third Debris Chute (sign). From the clearing, move toward a large metal drum by Lynn Creek (a rescue cache) and go LEFT on the *Cedar Mills Trail*, following signs to the parking lot. Budget about 1.5 hours for this 9.5 km advanced run. Note that *Headwaters Trail* is rarely dry and often choked with snow and mud well into the spring. This extension is only recommended between the months of May and November. Expect sloppy conditions, even in summer.

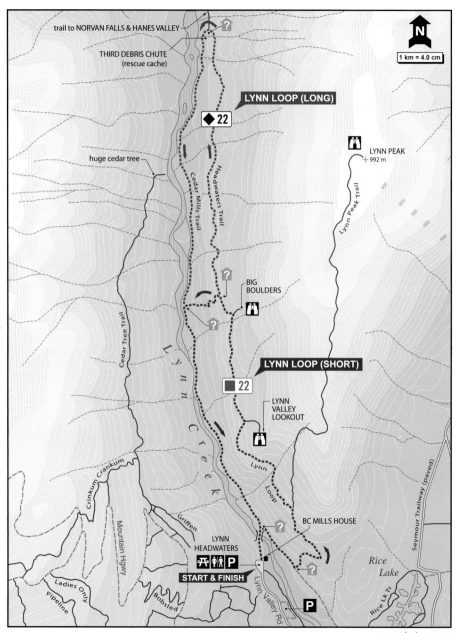

trail to NORVAN FALLS & HANES VALLEY

THIRD DEBRIS CHUTE
(rescue cache)

N

1 km = 4.0 cm

LYNN LOOP (LONG)

◆ 22

LYNN PEAK
+ 992 m

huge cedar tree

Cedar Mills Trail

Headwaters Trail

Lynn Peak Trail

800
700
600
500

BIG
BOULDERS

Cedar Tree Trail

LYNN LOOP (SHORT)

■ 22

Lynn Creek

LYNN
VALLEY
LOOKOUT

Lynn
Loop

Seymour Trailway (paved)

Crinkum Crankum

Griffen

BC MILLS HOUSE

Mountain Hwy

LYNN
HEADWATERS

Rice
Lake

Ladies Only
Pipeline

🏕️ 🚻 P

START & FINISH

Bobsled

Lynn Valley Rd

P

Rice Lk Tr

▲ 23 Hanes Valley ♥♥♥   15.6 km

STATS: 1091 m, August–October, TH: 10 U 497978 5467466

This epic pilgrimage tours through Lynn Headwaters and up to the Grouse Mountain Chalet via a steep and gnarly talus slope in the enchanted Hanes Valley. It gives stellar views of Coliseum and Crown mountains and provides an intense workout for advanced trail runners. From the Grouse Mountain Chalet, either descend the Skyride Gondola back to the base of the mountain or run down the *BCMC Trail* (descending the *Grouse Grind* is prohibited). Note that Hanes Valley typically hoards late-season snow and navigating through the talus is sketchy. Beware of a resident Sasquatch.

The Dirt

▸ From Lynn Headwaters parking area, run through the picnic area and across a bridge (Lynn Creek) to a large information kiosk. Turn LEFT and head up a gravel road adjacent to Lynn Creek. Keep LEFT past a junction for *Lynn Loop* and continue on *Cedar Mills Trail* to a huge clearing with a large metal container (a rescue cache). This is the Third Debris Chute.

▸ Head RIGHT through the clearing to a sign and turn LEFT onto *Headwaters Trail* toward Norvan Falls.

▸ When you reach Norvan Creek, stay LEFT (Norvan Falls is 100 m up to the right) and cross a metal suspension bridge. Continue following yellow markers to another sign and map. Go LEFT down to Lynn Creek and the *Hanes Valley* trail.

▸ Follow orange flagging across the creek before picking up a trail of yellow markers. Continue through the forest, slowly gaining elevation along *Hanes Valley*.

▸ Eventually, gain a clearing with a helicopter pad, rescue cache and sign at the base of a massive talus field. At the top left side of the talus is a prominent notch, Crown Pass. Aim for this feature as you scramble up the talus, following cairns and orange flagging.

▸ From Crown Pass, turn LEFT and follow steep and technical terrain all the way to Grouse Mountain. You'll pass trails to *Goat Mountain*, *Dam Mountain* and *Thunderbird Ridge*.

▸ Arrive at Grouse Mountain's upper zip line tower and stay RIGHT down the trail. Shortly, the trail starts to braid and may ▸▸

Access: Start at the main parking lot for Lynn Headwaters Regional Park. A car or taxi shuttle to Grouse Mountain is required beforehand.

To Get There: To make your car drop from downtown Vancouver, follow Route 99/1A (West Georgia Street) north across the Lions Gate Bridge and exit RIGHT into North Vancouver. At the first set of lights, turn LEFT on Capilano Road and drive 5.5 km uphill to the base of Grouse Mountain and park a car.

To get to Lynn Headwaters Regional Park from Grouse Mountain, drive down Capilano Road and enter Highway 1 heading EAST. Take Exit 19 for Lynn Valley. Follow Lynn Valley Road northeast for 3 km to the park entrance on the corner of Lynn Valley and Dempsey roads. Follow the narrow park road for 1 km to its end (two overflow parking lots are passed before you each the main parking lot).

Map: Page 129

Hanes Valley *Jonathan Wong cruising past Goat Mountain under glorious blue skies.*

Hanes Valley *From top: Tackling the heinous talus slope near Crown Pass; Hanes Valley, with Coliseum Mountain looming in the background; Crown Pass, with Crown Mountain on the left and Goat Mountain on the right.*

become confusing as you try to navigate the various options. Simply continue moving downhill toward Grouse Mountain and you'll be heading in the correct general direction.

▶ Duck under a pipeline and veer downhill to a large clearing at the end of a gravel service road that features a kiosk and notice board. Follow the gravel road past the grizzly pen to finish at Grouse Mountain Chalet. Time for a cheeseburger…

▶ From the Chalet, ride the gondola down to the base or tackle a knee-pounding descent down the *BCMC Trail* (*Grouse Grind* is closed to downhill traffic).

Variation: Pure masochists will likely feel compelled to run Hanes Valley as a complete loop starting and finishing at Lynn Headwaters. This will provide a painful, 27-kilometre run with an insane burl-factor, possibly the most difficult run in the book!

To execute this torture-fest, run Hanes Valley as described above. Once at the Grouse Mountain Chalet, descend the *BCMC Trail* (running down the *Grouse Grind* is prohibited). Turn LEFT onto the *Baden-Powell Trail* and run it all the way back to Lynn Valley (see Grouse Mountain to Lynn Headwaters description on page 118). Budget 5–6 hours for this experts-only journey.

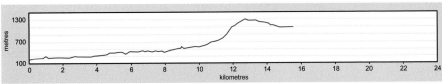

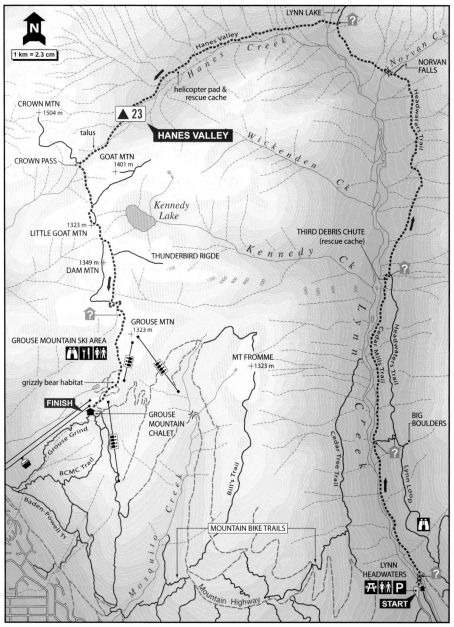

N

1 km = 2.3 cm

LYNN LAKE

Hanes Valley

Hanes Creek

Norvan Ck

NORVAN
FALLS

helicopter pad &
rescue cache

CROWN MTN
+ 1504 m

▲ 23

HANES VALLEY

talus

Wickenden Ck

Headwaters Trail

CROWN PASS

GOAT MTN
1401 m

Kennedy
Lake

1323 m

LITTLE GOAT MTN

THIRD DEBRIS CHUTE
(rescue cache)

1349 m
DAM MTN

THUNDERBIRD RIGDE

Kennedy

Ck

1200

1100
1000 900 800

900 800 700

GROUSE MTN
1323 m

Lynn

Creek

GROUSE MOUNTAIN SKI AREA

MT FROMME
+ 1323 m

Headwaters Trail

Cedar Mills Trail

grizzly bear habitat

BIG
BOULDERS

FINISH

GROUSE
MOUNTAIN
CHALET

Grouse Grind

BCMC Trail

Bill's Trail

Mosquito Creek

Cedar Tree Trail

Lynn Loop

Baden-Powell Tr

MOUNTAIN BIKE TRAILS

LYNN
HEADWATERS

Mountain Highway

START

www.richwheater.com

◆ 24 Tour de Lynn ♥   26.6 km

STATS: 404 m, May–November, TH: 10 U 498442 5463542

This run is another miniature epic that explores some of the finest technical trails and rainforest on the North Shore. You'll negotiate a constant barrage of obstacles while passing waterfalls, creeks and the famously-treacherous Lynn Canyon. Man-eating mud pits and gargantuan root systems are the name of the game as you claw your way to Norvan Falls and back.

The Dirt

▸ From the north end of Inter River Park (by sports field #8) , head NORTH past a gate and down a short road. Turn RIGHT onto a wide path that narrows and becomes the *Lillooet Trail* (a.k.a. the *Sea-to-Sky Trail*). ➤➤

Access: Start at the north end of Inter River Park in North Vancouver.

To Get There: If approaching from the EAST on Highway 1, take Exit 22A for Lillooet Road. At the traffic lights, turn LEFT and head up Lillooet Road. Continue about 100 m past Purcell Way (Capilano University) and turn LEFT on Inter River Road. At the T-intersection, turn RIGHT and find parking at the far (north) end of the sports fields.

If approaching from the WEST on Highway 1, take Exit 22 for Mount Seymour Parkway. At the traffic lights, turn LEFT toward Capilano University/Lillooet Road and drive to a second set of traffic lights. Continue STRAIGHT up Lillooet Road and approach the parking area as per the directions in the previous paragraph.

Map: Pages 134-135

Tour de Lynn *Left to right: Boardwalk bridge slick with rain on the upper Lynn Loop trail; Andrew Fodor runs the upper Lynn Loop trail.*

▸ Run uphill to a sign and turn LEFT onto the *Baden-Powell Trail*. Descend to a long boardwalk over a marsh and continue up to a large bridge over Twin Falls. Turn LEFT, cross the bridge and climb a staircase to a large clearing. Turn RIGHT and follow the trail to a paved parking area (the Lynn Canyon Ecology Centre).

▸ Keep RIGHT through the parking area for 50 m to the Suspension Bridge. Immediately before the bridge, turn LEFT onto the *Baden-Powell Trail* and descend steps. Follow boardwalks and climb a steep staircase to reach Lynn Valley Road (and coffee shop).

▸ Turn RIGHT, follow the road for 50 m and go RIGHT down Rice Lake Road. Keep to the LEFT (do NOT cross the bridge) past houses then get onto the *Varley Trail* and follow it to the Lynn Headwaters main parking area. Continue through the picnic area and cross a bridge over Lynn Creek to a large junction and map kiosk.

▸ Turn RIGHT and run the gravel road to another map kiosk and junction. Go LEFT onto *Lynn Loop* and run 2.5 km past trails to *Lynn Peak*, *Lynn Valley Lookout* and *Big Boulders*.

▸ Just past *Big Boulders* is a junction. Stay RIGHT and follow the *Headwaters Trail* to the Third Debris Chute (a huge clearing). This stretch is FAR nastier than *Lynn Loop* and often choked with snow well into the spring.

▸ Keep RIGHT along *Headwaters Trail* to Norvan Creek and look for a sign leading RIGHT to Norvan Falls (150 m). Check out the waterfall, then turn around and head back to the Third Debris Chute. ▸▸

▶ At the clearing, head RIGHT toward a large metal container (the rescue cache) and turn LEFT onto *Cedar Mills Trail,* which leads back to the parking and picnic areas.

▶ Continue through the parking area and take the *Varley Trail* to the Pipe Bridge on Rice Lake Road. Cross the bridge and immediately turn RIGHT into the forest. Keep RIGHT and descend a massive staircase to a large pool in the creek.

▶ From the pool, continue LEFT toward the Capilano Suspension Bridge. At the bridge junction, go LEFT (now the *Baden-Powell Trail*) for 25 m and continue RIGHT toward Twin Falls.

▶ At Twin Falls, keep LEFT on the *Baden-Powell Trail* and cross the long boardwalk over the marsh. Charge up the stout little hill to join the *Lillooet Trail* (sign). Turn RIGHT and run back to Inter River Park. Stretch, then enjoy a well-deserved beer and a side of Yorkshire pudding at Seymour's Pub at the base of Lillooet Road.

"The best runner leaves no tracks." - Tao Te Ching

Tour de Lynn *Counterclockwise from top left: Historic BC Mills House; Lynn Creek as seen from the bridge at the Lynn Headwaters base area; information kiosk by the bridge crossing; Andrew Fodor on the Lynn Loop switchbacks.*

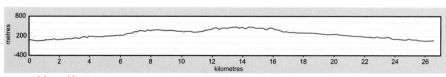

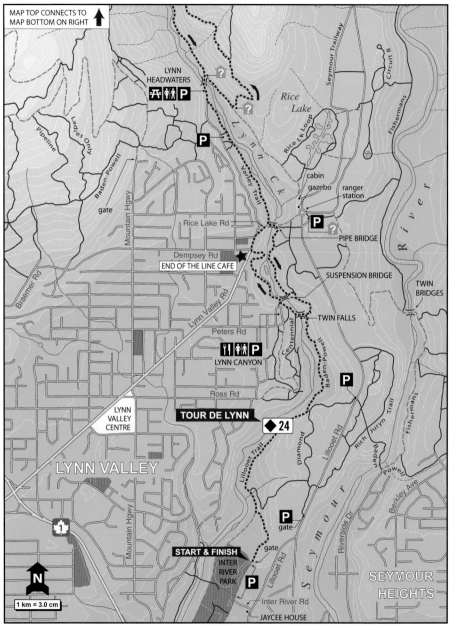

MAP TOP CONNECTS TO
MAP BOTTOM ON RIGHT

LYNN
HEADWATERS

Pipeline

Ladies Only

Baden-Powell

Mountain Hgwy

gate

Rice Lake Rd

Braemar Rd

Dempsey Rd
END OF THE LINE CAFE

Lynn Valley Rd

Peters Rd

LYNN CANYON

Ross Rd

LYNN
VALLEY
CENTRE

TOUR DE LYNN

◆ 24

Lillooet Trail

LYNN VALLEY

Mountain Hgwy

START & FINISH
INTER
RIVER
PARK

P
gate

gate

Lillooet Rd

Inter River Rd
JAYCEE HOUSE

N

1 km = 3.0 cm

L y n n   C r e e k

Lynn Valley Trail

Rice Lake

Rice Lk Loop

cabin
gazebo
ranger
station

PIPE BRIDGE

SUSPENSION BRIDGE

TWIN FALLS

Centennial

Baden-Powell

Diamond

Lillooet Rd

Seymour Trailway

Circuit 8

Fishermans

R i v e r

TWIN
BRIDGES

Fishermans

Rich Juryn Trail

Baden-Powell

Riverside Dr

Berkley Ave

SEYMOUR
HEIGHTS

S e y m o u r

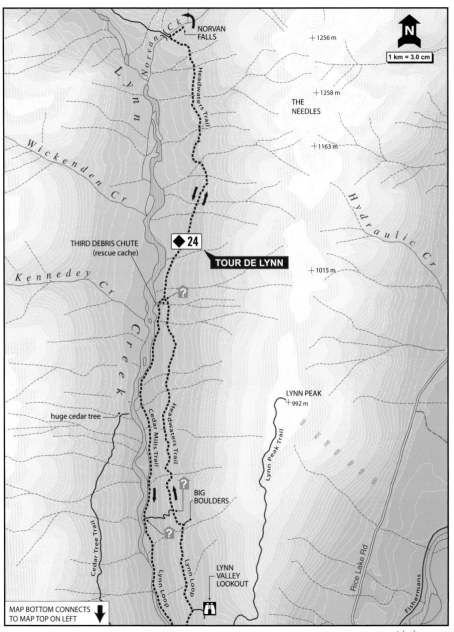

N

1 km = 3.0 cm

+ 1256 m

+ 1258 m

THE
NEEDLES

+ 1163 m

NORVAN
FALLS

Lynn

Norvan Ck

Headwaters Trail

Wickenden Cr

Hydraulic Cr

◆ 24

THIRD DEBRIS CHUTE
(rescue cache)

TOUR DE LYNN

+ 1015 m

Kennedey Cr

Creek

?

LYNN PEAK
+ 992 m

huge cedar tree

Cedar Mills Trail

Headwaters Trail

Lynn Peak Trail

600
800
700
400
500
300

BIG
BOULDERS

?

?

Cedar Tree Trail

Lynn Loop

Lynn Loop

LYNN
VALLEY
LOOKOUT

Rice Lake Rd

Fishermans

MAP BOTTOM CONNECTS
TO MAP TOP ON LEFT

◆ 25 Lynn
Headwaters to Deep Cove ♥♥♥   12.5 km

STATS: 408 m, April–November, TH (Lynn Valley): 10 U 498340 5466100

This arduous journey follows the *Baden-Powell Trail* from Lynn Valley to Deep Cove. It's packed with technical terrain and includes the notorious Seymour Grind, a backbreaking climb from the Seymour River to the top of *Severed Dick* (a.k.a. *Good Samaritan*). Expect many staircases and boardwalks, some easy gravel sections and plenty of obstacles to dodge and hurdle. The scenic Panorama Park welcomes you to Deep Cove, home of legendary donuts at Honey's Café.

The Dirt

▶ From End of the Line General Store, cross the street to the *Baden-Powell Trail*. Head downhill to Lynn Creek, run the creek side for a bit and climb steps to the Lynn Canyon Suspension Bridge.

▶ Cross the bridge and turn RIGHT on the other side. Run for 50 m and bear RIGHT at a sign for the Twin Falls. Follow the trail down lots of stairs.

▶ Keep LEFT past Twin Falls (do NOT cross the bridge). Continue downhill on the *Baden-Powell Trail*, cross a long boardwalk and tackle a short, steep hill to a junction with *Lillooet Trail* (sign). Turn LEFT and continue along the *Baden-Powell Trail* (passing an unmarked trail on the right) to Lillooet Road and a small parking lot.

▶ Cross the road to an impossible-to-miss sign for the *Baden-Powell Trail*. Continue along the *Baden-Powell Trail*, passing Lookout Hill and the *Richard Juryn Trail*.

▶ Continue STRAIGHT through a junction with Powerline Road & cross the power line. Descend switchbacks to the Seymour River.
▶▶

Access: *Start at the corner of Dempsey and Lynn Valley roads in North Vancouver. A taxi or car shuttle to Deep Cove is required beforehand.*

To Get There: *If travelling EAST on Highway 1, take Exit 22B for Mt Seymour Parkway; if travelling WEST, take Exit 22. Once off the freeway, follow Mt Seymour Parkway east for about 5 km, drop down a steep hill and turn LEFT onto Deep Cove Road. The road veers right to become Gallant Avenue in the village of Deep Cove. Turn LEFT on Panorama Drive and find parking at Panorama Park. Drop a car here.*

To get to the start of the run from Deep Cove, return to Highway 1 and enter the freeway heading WEST. Take Exit 19 for Lynn Valley and head east on Lynn Valley Road, following signs for Lynn Headwaters Regional Park. At the corner of Dempsey and Lynn Valley roads is End of the Line General Store and the entrance to the Baden-Powell Trail. Park here.

Map: *Pages 140–141*

Lynn Headwaters to Deep Cove
Clockwise from left: An enjoyable stretch of Baden-Powell trail; Lynn Canyon Suspension Bridge; sign pointing the way on Indian River Road.

▶ Cross a bridge over Seymour River to a large intersection at the end of Riverside Drive. Turn LEFT and head uphill for 100 m to a junction with *Fisherman's* (sign).

▶ Turn RIGHT and follow the *Baden-Powell Trail* up to Hyannis Drive. Cross Hyannis Drive and continue on the *Baden-Powell Trail* to a large rock step by the creek (sign). This is where the *Baden-Powell Trail* crosses over *Bridle Path*.

▶ Keep RIGHT for 50 m to an intersection and turn LEFT on the *Baden-Powell Trail*. After about 200 m, the trail begins to climb steeply up the Seymour Grind. This section is rough and, when wet, it's a virtual waterfall!

▶ At the obvious flat top-out is the junction with *Severed Dick*. Continue STRAIGHT on *Baden-Powell Trail* to a junction with the *Mushroom Trail*. Turn RIGHT (still on the *Baden-Powell Trail*) and follow a wide, rocky path for 1 km down to a junction with *Old Buck* (sign). Continue STRAIGHT for 50 m then turn RIGHT onto the *Baden-Powell Trail*.

▶ Head downhill and cross Mt Seymour Road to a small parking lot and information kiosk. Continue down the *Baden-Powell Trail* to Indian River Road.

▶ Go LEFT along Indian River Road for 500 m, turn RIGHT and follow the *Baden-Powell Trail* down to a clearing. Trend RIGHT across the power line and pick up a narrow, unmarked trail that leads past a rocky bluff. Just ahead is a great viewpoint (Quarry Rock), but stay RIGHT and continue on the *Baden-Powell Trail*.

▶ The trail goes up and down for a while before dropping steeply to Panorama Road. Turn RIGHT and run the sidewalk to Panorama Park.

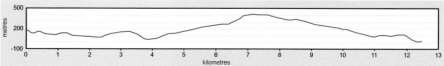

◆ 26 Dirty Duo Short ♥♥ 13.7 km

STATS: 129 m, March–November, TH: 10 U 498273 5462899

This fine excursion follows the 2010 Dirty Duo short racecourse and is a good objective for roadies looking to sample the wild side. The technical portion of the run is found along the *Diamond* and *Baden-Powell* trails, and offers a pleasant romp around lower Lynn Creek. The remainder of the journey grinds along gravel paths and service roads, leading past a tranquil stretch of the Seymour River and through misty rainforest.

The Dirt

▶ From Jaycee House, run up Lillooet Road past the equestrian center and chapel. Continue STRAIGHT through a large gate into the cemetery and run the main road to a short trail that connects back with Lillooet Road.

▶ Continue past parking lots and a yellow gate before turning LEFT onto the first wide gravel trail. Run 300 m to a junction and turn LEFT onto *Diamond* (yellow trail markers). This packed-gravel path soon turns into twisty singletrack with tons of mud!

▶ Follow *Diamond* to a junction with the *Baden-Powell Trail*. Turn LEFT, run a few paces to a sign, go RIGHT and descend the *Baden-Powell Trail* to a long boardwalk over a marsh. Continue uphill to Twin Falls and a bridge.

▶ Keep RIGHT past Twin Falls (do NOT cross the bridge) and continue up the *Baden-Powell Trail* to a junction with the *Suspension*

▶▶

Access: *Start and finish at Jaycee House (1251 Lillooet Road).*

To Get There: *If approaching from the EAST on Highway 1, take Exit 22A for Lillooet Road in North Vancouver. At the lights, turn LEFT and head up Lillooet Road, past Purcell Way (Capilano University), and turn LEFT on Inter River Park Road (Jaycee House is on the southwest corner). Continue a short distance to find parking at any of the sports fields.*

If approaching from the WEST on Highway 1, take Exit 22 for Mount Seymour Parkway. At the traffic lights, turn LEFT toward Capilano University/Lillooet Road and drive to a second set of traffic lights. Continue STRAIGHT up Lillooet Road, approaching Jaycee House as per the directions in the previous paragraph.

Map: *Pages 140–141*

Dirty Duo Short *Clockwise from left: Lower Seymour Conservation Reserve (LSCR) base area gazebo; a misty day highlights the majestic composition of the rainforest; Josie Hetyei cruising mellow terrain in the LSCR.*

Bridge Trail. Stay RIGHT and continue running uphill past a gigantic water treatment plant (on your right) and a short connector trail (on your left). Eventually, you'll reach the Lower Seymour Conservation Reserve (LSCR) central gazebo and roundabout.

▶ Turn RIGHT past the gazebo and information center to the main parking area and map kiosk. Continue past the parking area and through a fence-enclosed trail chute.

▶ After the chute, turn RIGHT (sign) and descend *Twin Bridges* (a gravel service road) to the Seymour River.

▶ At the river, turn LEFT on *Fisherman's* and run to a well-marked junction with *Homestead* (sign). Turn LEFT and grind up *Homestead*.

▶ At the top, turn RIGHT and retrace your steps through the chute to the central gazebo beyond the parking area.

▶ Stay LEFT past the gazebo and re-enter the *Suspension Bridge Trail.* Retrace this path until it merges with the *Baden-Powell Trail* at the suspension bridge turnoff. Stay LEFT and descend the *Baden-Powell Trail* past Twin Falls and cross the long boardwalk.

▶ Wrestle a short, nasty hill. At the top, turn LEFT for 25 m before turning RIGHT back onto *Diamond* (yellow markers). Follow *Diamond* to a junction and turn RIGHT toward the yellow gate at Lillooet Road. Head back through the cemetery to finish at Jaycee House.

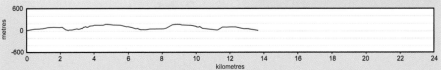

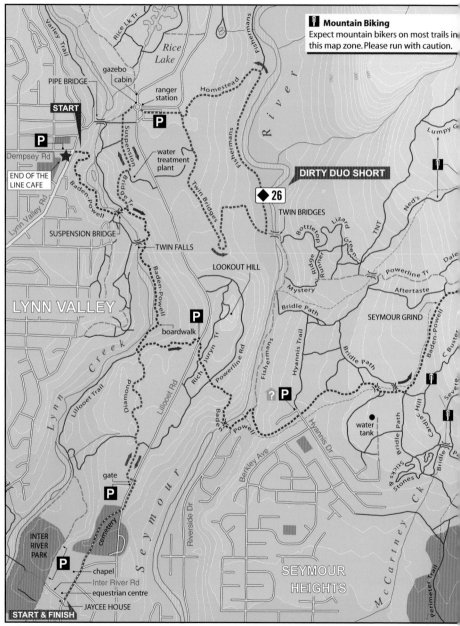

Mountain Biking
Expect mountain bikers on most trails in this map zone. Please run with caution.

DIRTY DUO SHORT

◆ 26

START

PIPE BRIDGE

P

END OF THE LINE CAFE

Dempsey Rd

P

Varley Trail

Rice Lk Tr

Rice Lake

gazebo cabin

ranger station

P

Homestead

Fishermans

River

Lumpy G

Ned's

Suspension Bridge Tr

Baden-Powell

water treatment plant

Twin Bridges

Fishermans

TWIN BRIDGES

Bottletop Ridge

Lizard Green

TNT

Dale

SUSPENSION BRIDGE

Lynn Valley Rd

TWIN FALLS

Baden-Powell

LOOKOUT HILL

Mystery

Bridle Path

Powerline Tr

Aftertaste

SEYMOUR GRIND

LYNN VALLEY

P

boardwalk

Rich Juryn Tr

Powerline Rd

Hyannis Trail

Bridle Path

Baden-Powell

C Buster

Lillooet Trail

Diamond

Lillooet Rd

Baden-Powell

Fishermans

? P

Hyannis Dr

water tank

Bridle Path

Cardiac Hill

Severe

Sticks & Stones

Creek

Lynn

Berkley Ave

gate

P

cemetery

Riverside Dr

Seymour

McCartney Ck

INTER RIVER PARK

P

chapel
Inter River Rd
equestrian centre
JAYCEE HOUSE

SEYMOUR HEIGHTS

Perimeter Trail

START & FINISH

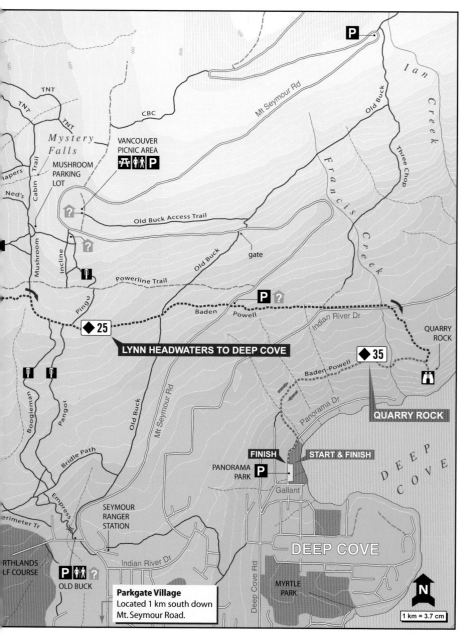

Ian Creek

Mt Seymour Rd

Old Buck

Three Chop

TNT
TNT
TNT
CBC

Mystery Falls

VANCOUVER PICNIC AREA

MUSHROOM PARKING LOT

Francis Creek

Ned's

Cabin Trail

Shapers

Old Buck Access Trail

Mushroom

Incline

Old Buck

gate

Powerline Trail

Pingu

Baden Powell

P

QUARRY ROCK

◆ 25

LYNN HEADWATERS TO DEEP COVE

Indian River Dr

Baden-Powell

◆ 35

Boogieman

Pangot

QUARRY ROCK

Panorama Dr

Mt Seymour Rd

Old Buck

Bridle Path

FINISH

START & FINISH

DEEP COVE

Empress

PANORAMA PARK

Gallant

Perimeter Tr

SEYMOUR RANGER STATION

RTHLANDS LF COURSE

Indian River Dr

Deep Cove Rd

DEEP COVE

OLD BUCK

MYRTLE PARK

N

Parkgate Village
Located 1 km south down
Mt. Seymour Road.

1 km = 3.7 cm

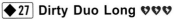
STATS: 452 m, March–December, TH: 10 U 498273 5462899

This grueling safari is sure to make your ankles groan. The route follows an attractive circuit around Lynn Creek, the Lower Seymour Conservation Reserve (LSCR) and the dank slopes of Mount Seymour. It features everything from flat gravel paths to snarled and muddy singletrack. Plenty of flow is found along a number of enjoyable sections, but many will suffer the burn up *Old Buck* and the punishing descent down *Ned's Atomic Dustbin* (a.k.a. *Ned's*) and *Bottletop*.

Access: Same as for Dirty Duo Short.

Map: Pages 144–145

The Dirt

▶ From Jaycee House, head down Inter River Park Road on the sidewalk and turn LEFT at the first road by the first sports field. Go 50 m and turn RIGHT onto a vague path that leads between the fields. After 100 m, veer RIGHT onto a trail before heading LEFT down toward Lynn Creek and a bridge.

▶ Turn RIGHT and follow the wide gravel path for 800 m. Keep LEFT and head up the *Lillooet Trail* to a junction with the *Baden-Powell Trail*. Turn LEFT and descend steep gnar to a slippery boardwalk. Continue uphill to Twin Falls and a bridge.

▶ Keep RIGHT past Twin Falls (do NOT cross the bridge) and follow the *Baden-Powell Trail* up to a junction with the *Suspension Bridge Trail*. Stay RIGHT and continue uphill, passing a water filtration plant on your right and a couple of short trails leading to the Pipe Bridge on your left. Eventually reach the LSCR central gazebo and roundabout.

▶ From the gazebo, turn RIGHT and run past an information center and main parking area before entering a fenced chute.

▶ After the chute, turn RIGHT and descend *Twin Bridges* (a long gravel road) to the Seymour River. Cross the river, turn RIGHT and follow *Fisherman's* for 400 m. Pass *Bottletop* and *Mystery Creek Trail* en route to a junction with *Bridle Path* (sign).

▶ Turn LEFT and climb *Bridle Path* to a bench. Go LEFT on *Hyannis Connector* for 250 m to another junction with *Bridle Path* (sign). Turn RIGHT and follow *Bridle Path* all the way to *Old Buck* (near Mount Seymour Road). There are many minor trails along this section. Make sure to stay on *Bridle Path*. ▶▶

Dirty Duo Long *Navigating second-growth grunge on Mount Seymour (left) and a slick boardwalk on Ned's (above).*

▶ At *Old Buck,* turn LEFT and climb for 1 km to a junction with the *Baden-Powell Trail.* Turn LEFT and follow the *Baden-Powell Trail* past a couple of mountain bike trail entrances on the left, to a signed junction with *Mushroom Trail.* Stay RIGHT and continue up to and across the power line. Continue up *Mushroom Trail* to an obvious fork. Go RIGHT 25 m to the historic Mushroom Parking Lot, which is now just an overgrown stump.

▶ From the Mushroom Parking Lot, turn LEFT and run 5 m to a sign. Go RIGHT and immediately reach a fork. Turn LEFT onto the mountain bike trail, *Ned's* (orange marker on tree). Make a lengthy descent of *Ned's* to an unmarked junction with *Bottletop.* Turn RIGHT and run 100 m before going LEFT up a short hill to Nuggie's Bench. Keep to the RIGHT along *Bottletop* before descending to *Fisherman's.*

▶ Turn RIGHT on *Fisherman's* and cross a large bridge over the Seymour River. Immediately turn RIGHT and follow *Fisherman's* to *Homestead* (sign). Turn LEFT and labor up *Homestead.* At the top, turn RIGHT and run through the fenced chute to the LSCR central gazebo, which is beyond the parking area.

▶ Pass the gazebo and turn LEFT onto the *Suspension Bridge Trail.* Follow the main trail to a junction with the *Baden-Powell Trail* (sign). Keep LEFT and descend the *Baden-Powell Trail* past Twin Falls to the long boardwalk over the marsh.

▶ Climb a short, burly hill to a junction with the *Lillooet Trail* (sign). Turn LEFT on the *Baden-Powell Trail* and run for 25 m before going RIGHT onto *Diamond* (yellow markers).

▶ Follow *Diamond* to a T-junction and turn RIGHT toward Lillooet Road. Stay RIGHT along Lillooet Road, passing the yellow gate and parking areas. Take a short trail into the cemetery and run the central cemetery road back to Lillooet Road and Jaycee House.

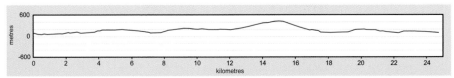

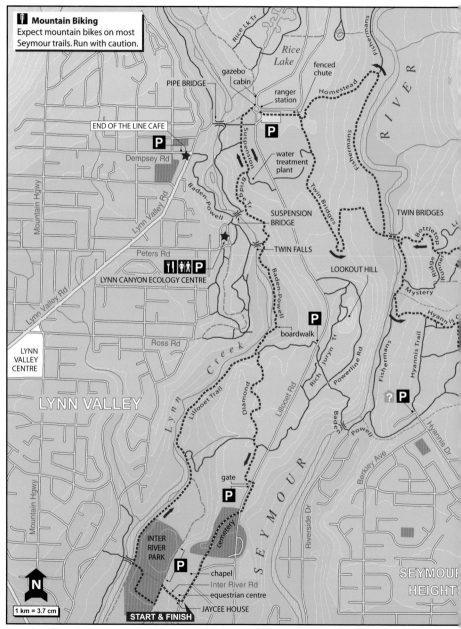

Mountain Biking

Expect mountain bikes on most Seymour trails. Run with caution.

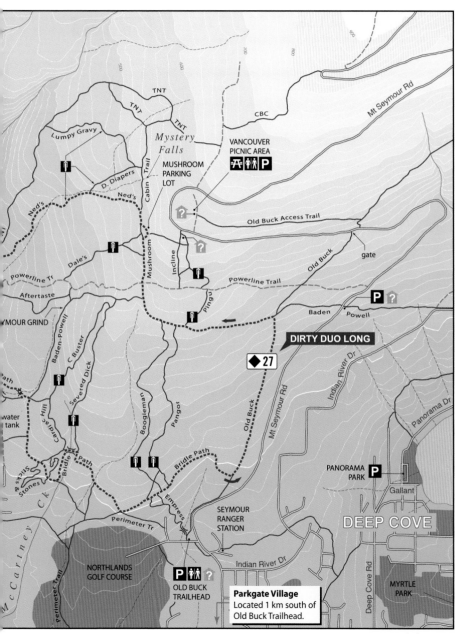

■ 28 Richard Juryn Loop   5.3 km

STATS: 98 m, Year-round, TH: 10 U 498273 5462899

This mini-mission links relatively flat sections of the forested *Diamond*, *Baden-Powell* and *Richard Juryn* trails in the Lower Seymour Conservation Reserve (LSCR). It's a good introduction to intermediate trails and can be especially challenging when wet due to an abundance of mud pits. Be careful not to lose a shoe.

Access: *Same as for Dirty Duo Short.*

Map: *Pages 148–149*

The Dirt

▶ From Jaycee House, head up the west (left) side of Lillooet Road past the equestrian center. Follow brown *Richard Juryn Trail* signposts past the chapel and head STRAIGHT up the paved road into the cemetery.

▶ Run the cemetery road to its end and pick up a short trail that leads to Lillooet Road. Follow Lillooet Road north, passing some small parking areas on the left. At a large yellow gate (the first entrance to *Diamond*), cross the road to a map kiosk. Run north along the roadside trail for 200 m. Turn LEFT and cross the road and enter *Diamond* trail, identified by yellow tree markers. ▶▶

Variation: You can shorten this run to approximately 30 minutes by starting at the small parking areas on Lillooet Road near the yellow LSCR entrance gate. This eliminates 2 km of road running and the cemetery section, which reduces the total length of the outing to 3.5 km

Richard Juryn Loop *Clockwise from bottom left: Sword ferns line the trail; Lillooet Road and the entrance gate to the Lower Seymour Conservation Reserve; yellow Diamond Trail tree markers; mellow section of the Baden-Powell trail.*

▶ Run *Diamond* to the first junction and turn RIGHT. The friendly gravel surface soon gives way to more technical ground with lots of mud, slippery roots and boardwalks. The trail weaves through a beautiful forest full of moss-coated trees.

▶ At a junction with the *Baden-Powell Trail,* turn RIGHT and run to a small parking area on Lillooet Road. Cross the road and continue up the *Baden-Powell Trail*, which is marked by an impossible-to-miss sign. After 100 m, turn RIGHT and head down the *Richard Juryn Trail* (sign). Descend to a gravel service road.

▶ At the road, turn LEFT, run 100 m, go RIGHT and follow the *Richard Juryn Trail* under the power lines back to Lillooet Road. Cross the road and re-enter *Diamond*. At a three-way junction, go LEFT and follow the gravel trail back to Lillooet Road.

▶ Turn RIGHT and head down Lillooet Road for 100 m past the small parking lots. Go RIGHT onto the short trail into the cemetery, run through the cemetery to Lillooet Road and back to Jaycee House at Inter River Drive.

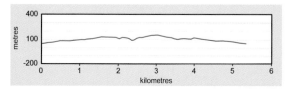

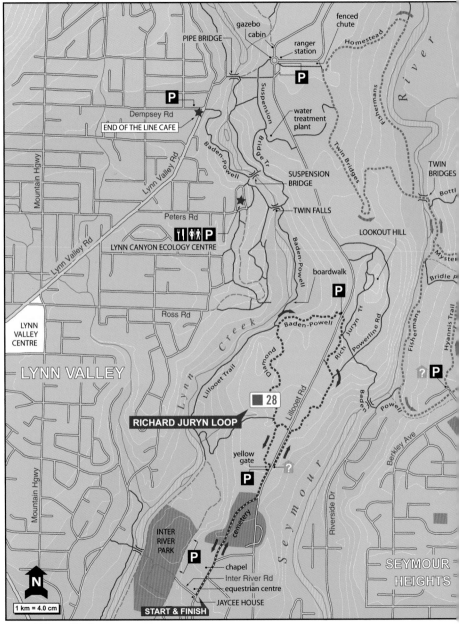

fenced chute

gazebo cabin

PIPE BRIDGE

ranger station

Homestead

River

P

Suspension

water treatment plant

END OF THE LINE CAFE

Dempsey Rd

P

Baden-Powell

Bridge Tr

Fishermans

Twin Bridges

TWIN BRIDGES

SUSPENSION BRIDGE

Bottl

Peters Rd

TWIN FALLS

LOOKOUT HILL

Mountain Hwy

Lynn Valley Rd

LYNN CANYON ECOLOGY CENTRE

P

Mystery

Bridle p

boardwalk

P

Baden-Powell

Ross Rd

Baden-Powell

Rich Juryn Tr

Powerline Rd

Fishermans

Hyannis Trail

LYNN VALLEY CENTRE

Lynn Valley Rd

LYNN VALLEY

Creek

Lynn

Lillooet Trail

Diamond

28

RICHARD JURYN LOOP

Lillooet Rd

Baden

Powell

Berkley Ave

? P

yellow gate

P

?

Seymour

Riverside Dr

SEYMOUR HEIGHTS

Mountain Hwy

INTER RIVER PARK

cemetery

P

chapel

Inter River Rd

equestrian centre

JAYCEE HOUSE

START & FINISH

N

1 km = 4.0 cm

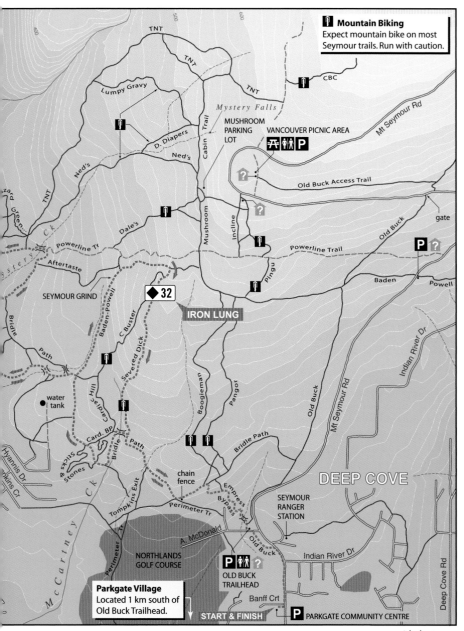

Mountain Biking
Expect mountain bike on most Seymour trails. Run with caution.

TNT

CBC

Lumpy Gravy

Mystery Falls

MUSHROOM PARKING LOT

VANCOUVER PICNIC AREA

Mt Seymour Rd

D. Diapers

Ned's

Cabin Trail

Old Buck Access Trail

Ned's

TNT

Mushroom

Old Buck

gate

zard Green...

Dale's

Incline

Powerline Trail

Old Buck

Ck

Powerline Tr

Pingu

Baden

Powell

Aftertaste

Mystery

◆ 32

IRON LUNG

SEYMOUR GRIND

Baden-Powell

C Buster

Bridle

Path

Severed Dick

Boogieman

Pangor

Old Buck

Mt Seymour Rd

Indian River Dr

water tank

Calcipel Hill

Card. BP

Bridle Path

Bridle Path

Sticks & Stones

Path

Empress Bypass

DEEP COVE

Tompkins Exit

Perimeter Tr

Perimeter Tr

chain fence

SEYMOUR RANGER STATION

McCartney Ck

Hyannis Dr

pkins Cr

A. McDonald

Old Buck

NORTHLANDS GOLF COURSE

OLD BUCK TRAILHEAD

Indian River Dr

Deep Cove Rd

Parkgate Village
Located 1 km south of Old Buck Trailhead.

Banff Crt

START & FINISH

PARKGATE COMMUNITY CENTRE

■ 29 LSCR Canyon Loop 5.1 km

STATS: 88 m, Year-round, TH: 10 U 498917 5466414

You'll be hard-pressed to find a better route for greenhorns. This one starts off easy, but soon features basic root wrangling and rock hopping along the *Varley* and *Suspension Bridge* trails. Wide gravel paths and boardwalks connect the rough stuff offering great variety given a relatively short distance. To pique your interest, the Pipe Bridge provides a nauseating view into the deadly canyon below – a sobering reminder to stay away from the cliffs!

The Dirt

▶ From the parking lot map kiosk, follow the paved path west across the road (Rice Lake gate) to the central gazebo. Head RIGHT for a few paces to the Learning Lodge building and continue on a wide trail, the *Lynn Headwaters Connector*, toward Rice Lake.

▶ Stay LEFT past two Rice Lake turnoffs and another for *Lynn Loop* (map kiosk), before reaching a major junction with the *Cedar Mills Trail* (map kiosk).

▶ Turn LEFT and cross a bridge over Lynn Creek that leads to the Lynn Headwaters Park entrance and parking lot. From here, follow the *Varley Trail* to Rice Lake Road. Continue STRAIGHT past houses for 200 m, turn LEFT and cross the Pipe Bridge over Lynn Creek.

▶ After crossing the bridge, immediately turn RIGHT onto the unmarked *Suspension Bridge Trail*. Stay RIGHT and follow a never-ending staircase down to a large pool. Run along a boulder and root-strewn trail to a boardwalk and junction with the *Baden-Powell Trail* by the Lynn Canyon Suspension Bridge.

▶ Stay LEFT for 25 m on the *Baden-Powell Trail* before turning LEFT again onto the upper portion of the *Suspension Bridge Trail*. Follow the main trail past a water-filtration plant and back to the central gazebo and Rice Lake gate. From here, go RIGHT past the information center and back to the parking area.

Access: Start at the Rice Lake parking lot in North Vancouver.

To Get There: If approaching from the EAST on Highway 1, take Exit 22A for Lillooet Road. At the lights, turn LEFT and head up Lillooet Road, past Purcell Way (Capilano University), for 4.6 km to the Lower Seymour Conservation Reserve (LSCR). You'll pass by the massive Seymour-Capilano water-filtration plant before turning RIGHT into a parking lot at the Rice Lake base area.

If approaching from the WEST on Highway 1, take Exit 22 for Mount Seymour Parkway. At the traffic lights, turn LEFT toward Capilano University/Lillooet Road and drive to a second set of traffic lights. Continue STRAIGHT up Lillooet Road and approach Rice Lake as per the directions in the previous paragraph.

Map: Page 151

Variation: From the *Lynn Headwaters Connector*, turn RIGHT at the first turnoff to Rice Lake and run *Rice Lake Loop*, which reconnects with the *Lynn Headwaters Connector* after 2 km. This pleasant variation increases the total distance of the run to 7 km and provides access to the picturesque Rice Lake.

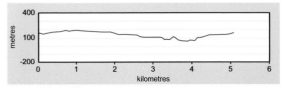

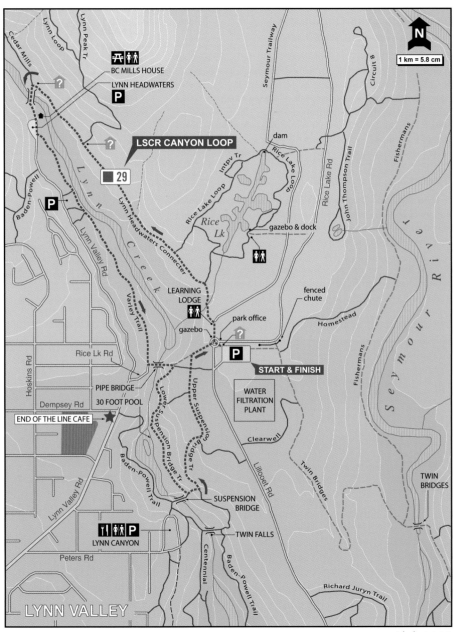

LSCR CANYON LOOP

29

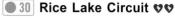

● 30 | Rice Lake Circuit ♥♥ 9.9 km

STATS: 135 m, Year-round, TH: 10 U 498917 5466414

This workout follows a figure eight loop around the Lower Seymour Conservation Reserve (LSCR). After descending *Twin Bridges* (a service road) you'll charge alongside the Seymour River and pass a mysterious tunnel before making a lung-searing ascent up *Homestead*. The second half is much more fun, as you cruise around scenic Rice Lake and make your return along the flowing *Varley Trail*. You can easily run this as two separate halves; if you do, I would recommend avoiding the *Twin Bridges–Homestead* section.

Access: Same as for the LSCR Canyon Loop on page 150.

Map: Page 155

The Dirt

▶ From the parking lot, head east through a chain-link fence chute to a junction with *Homestead* and *Twin Bridges*. Keep RIGHT and descend *Twin Bridges* (a service road) to a junction with *Fisherman's* at a blue bridge on the Seymour River.

▶ Turn LEFT and run *Fisherman's* past a tunnel and fisheries enhancement project (on the left) to a well-marked junction with *Homestead*. ▶▶

Rice Lake Circuit *From left: Boardwalk along the interpretive side trail that branches off Rice Lake Loop; water reflection on Rice Lake.*

Rice Lake Circuit *Left to right: Lady Fern frond; Western Redcedar bark; Western Hemlock bark.*

▶ Turn LEFT and slog up *Homestead*. At the top, go RIGHT through the fenced chute and return to the parking lot. Pass the parking lot and map kiosk, cross the road and pass the park office en route to the central gazebo.

▶ From the gazebo, go RIGHT toward the Learning Lodge. Follow a wide gravel path (the *Lynn Headwaters Connector*) toward Rice Lake and, at the first junction, turn RIGHT onto *Rice Lake Loop*.

▶ At the next junction, turn RIGHT and continue around *Rice Lake Loop* to a large clearing with toilets, a gazebo and a fishing deck. Veer left and pick up *Rice Lake Loop* immediately RIGHT of the gazebo. Continue around the lake and pass an exit to the paved *Seymour Valley Trailway*.

▶ At an unmarked fork, go RIGHT along an interpretive side trail until it rejoins the main *Rice Lake Loop*. At the next junction, go RIGHT and run to an intersection with *Lynn Headwaters Connector* (a gravel service road).

▶ Turn RIGHT and follow the gravel road past a map kiosk and a *Lynn Loop* trail entrance to a major intersection and information kiosk (Lynn Headwaters Regional Park). Turn LEFT and cross the bridge over Lynn Creek.

▶ Run through the picnic area and pick up the *Varley Trail* (sign) at the parking lot. Run the *Varley Trail* to Rice Lake Road and continue past houses. Turn LEFT and cross the Pipe Bridge. Continue STRAIGHT uphill to the LSCR gazebo and back to parking lot.

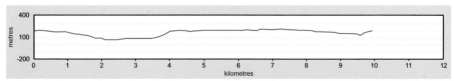

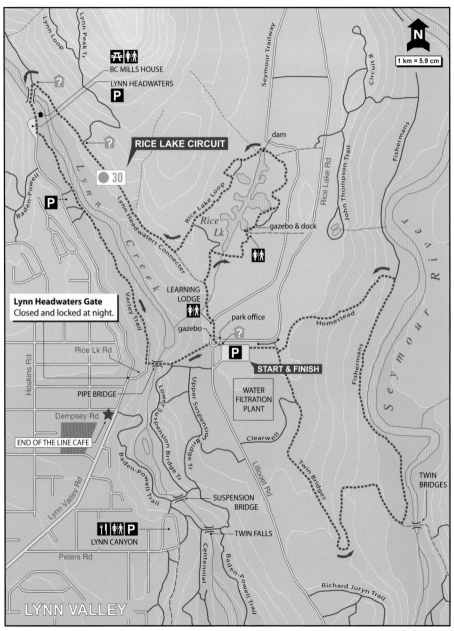

N

1 km = 5.9 cm

BC MILLS HOUSE
LYNN HEADWATERS
P

RICE LAKE CIRCUIT

dam

30

Rice Lake Loop

Rice Lk

gazebo & dock

Lynn Creek

Lynn Headwaters Connecter

Baden-Powell

P

Varley Trail

Seymour Trailway

Circuit 8

Fishermans

Rice Lake Rd

John Thompson Trail

Seymour River

Fishermans

LEARNING LODGE

gazebo

park office

Lynn Headwaters Gate
Closed and locked at night.

Rice Lk Rd

Hoskins Rd

PIPE BRIDGE

Dempsey Rd

END OF THE LINE CAFE

Lower Suspension Bridge Tr

Upper Suspension Bridge Tr

P
START & FINISH

WATER
FILTRATION
PLANT

Clearwell

Homestead

Fishermans

Twin Bridges

TWIN
BRIDGES

Lynn Valley Rd

Baden-Powell Trail

SUSPENSION
BRIDGE

Lillooet Rd

LYNN CANYON
P

TWIN FALLS

Peters Rd

Centennial

Baden-Powell Trail

Richard Juryn Trail

LYNN VALLEY

◆ 31 Hallows Eve   ♥♥ 20.6 km

STATS: 313 m, March–November, TH: 10 U 498273 5462899

This is a great circuit that tours the awesome Lynn Creek trails and takes a sneaky side trip to Mount Fromme. Most of the route covers typical North Shore terrain. Several taxing hills must be conquered, but don't despair – significant stretches of easy mileage give a welcome reprieve.

Access: Same as for Dirty Duo Short on page 138.

Map: Page 159

The Dirt

▸ From Jaycee House, run up the west (left) side of Lillooet Road passing the equestrian center and chapel. Continue STRAIGHT up the paved road through the cemetery to a short trail that connects back to Lillooet Road.

▸ Continue past some small parking areas and a large yellow gate before turning LEFT onto *Diamond*. Run 300 m to a junction and turn LEFT. The gravel surface soon becomes more technical as you follow yellow diamond-shaped tree markers.

▸ At the junction with the *Baden-Powell Trail*, turn LEFT and run 25 m to a signpost. Turn RIGHT and descend the *Baden-Powell Trail* to a long boardwalk over a marsh. Continue up to a bridge over Twin Falls.

▸ Do NOT cross the bridge. Instead, veer RIGHT and continue up the *Baden-Powell Trail* to a junction. Turn LEFT toward the *Suspension Bridge Trail* for 50 m, go RIGHT (just before the bridge) and follow a trail to 30 Foot Pool and an enormous staircase.

▸ Climb the exhausting staircase. At the top, go LEFT along the lower portion of the *Suspension Bridge Trail* to the Pipe Bridge over Lynn Creek. Cross the bridge and turn RIGHT onto Rice Lake Road. Run 100 m to the entrance to the *Varley Trail* (sign) and follow this path to the Lynn Headwaters Park parking area.

▸ From the parking area, turn back LEFT along the road and run 50 m before going RIGHT onto the *Baden-Powell Trail* (sign). Climb a steep staircase and continue up the *Baden-Powell Trail* past exits for *Griffin*, *McNair* and *Immonator*, until you reach Mountain Highway (a gravel service road).

▸ At Mountain Highway, turn RIGHT and run 400 m to a large

▸▸

Hallows Eve *Counterclockwise from below: Beware the creekside cliffs; the clear waters of Lynn Creek; Agata Zurek enjoying the lower Suspension Bridge trail.*

green water tank, map kiosk and toilets. Continue up the road past a gate for 500 m to the wide, gravel *Cedar Tree Trail* (sign) on the RIGHT. Follow this trail for 25 m before turning RIGHT onto *Griffin*, marked by a partially hidden, large wooden sign up in a tree.

▶ Run down *Griffin*, keeping LEFT at all junctions, to an intersection with the *Baden-Powell Trail*. Turn LEFT and follow the *Baden-Powell Trail* down a staircase to Lynn Headwaters Park Road. Turn LEFT and run back to the main parking area.

▶ Continue through the picnic area and cross a bridge over Lynn Creek to arrive at a major intersection and map kiosk. Stay LEFT and run a wide gravel path for 1.8 km toward the *Cedar Mills Trail*.

▶ At the *Cedar Mills Trail* junction (sign), turn RIGHT and climb steep switchbacks. At the top, turn RIGHT and follow the *Lynn Loop* for 2.5 km to a gravel road and map kiosk for the *Lynn Headwaters Connector*.

▶ Turn LEFT and run the gravel road for about 1 km, passing turnoffs for Rice Lake, to the Lower Seymour Conservation Reserve base area. Pass a wooden building (the Learning Lodge) and keep RIGHT past the central gazebo to a trail entrance with a signpost.

▶ Follow signs toward the *Suspension Bridge Trail* and Twin Falls, avoiding all other trails. At the turnoff to the Lynn Canyon Suspension Bridge, keep LEFT down the *Baden-Powell Trail* toward the bridge at Twin Falls. Stay LEFT past Twin Falls then run across the long boardwalk over the marsh. Next, battle a stout little hill.

▶ At the top, turn LEFT and run 25 m before heading RIGHT on *Diamond*. Follow this to an obvious junction and go RIGHT toward Lillooet Road. Run past parking pullouts and back through the cemetery to finish at Jaycee House.

Hallows Eve *From top: Descending the Griffin switchbacks; an elaborate sign chained to a tree marks the start of the Griffin trail.*

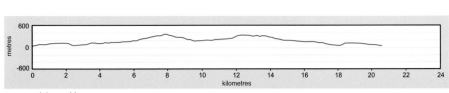

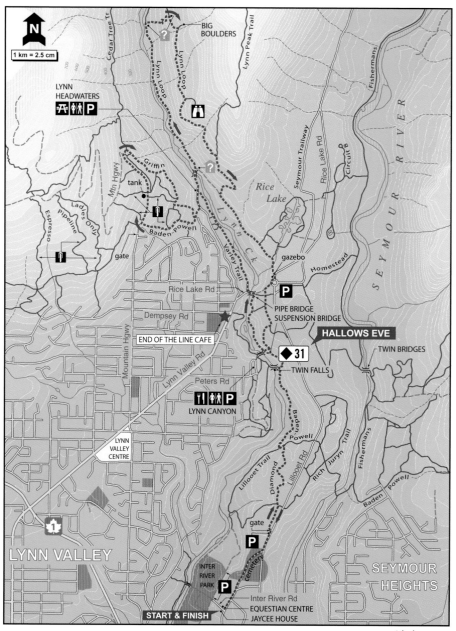

The Iron Lung is not a trail per se, but the title of an old racecourse. It's a high-quality circuit that sports three draining hill climbs, including the infamous Seymour Grind, which comes near the end when you least need it. The route begins at Parkgate Community Center and connects numerous well-traveled trails as you meander around the lower slopes of Mount Seymour. A proud tour of duty!

The Dirt

▶ From Parkgate Community Center, cross Banff Court, head up the left side of Mount Seymour Road to a sign and turn LEFT onto *Old Buck*. A short distance ahead, cross the road (Anne McDonald Way), run through the *Old Buck* parking lot and continue up the trail through two speed control gates.

▶ At the first junction, turn LEFT onto *Empress Bypass* (sign). Cross a bridge and labor up switchbacks (past the *Empress* exit) to *Bridle Path*. Watch for speeding mountain bikers!

▶ Turn LEFT on *Bridle Path* and run to a chain-link fence near Northlands Golf Course. Veer RIGHT and continue up *Bridle Path*. Stay to the RIGHT past a trail leading down to Tompkins Crescent.

▶ At a junction with *Severed Dick* (a.k.a. *Good Samaritan*), turn LEFT and cross a bridge then immediately turn LEFT and descend. At the bottom of this hill, keep RIGHT past a couple of vague trails (leading left) and climb back up *Bridle Path* to where *Cardiac Bypass* merges in from the right (easy to miss). Continue LEFT along the *Bridle Path* to a junction with the *Baden-Powell Trail*.

▶ Turn LEFT onto the *Baden-Powell Trail* and run 50 m to a rock step at a creek (sign). Stay LEFT down the *Baden-Powell Trail* all the way to Hyannis Drive. At Hyannis Drive, turn RIGHT and run 75 m to the *Hyannis Trail* entrance and map kiosk. Follow the wide trail, past two *Bridle Path* junctions, all the way to the power line.

▶▶

Access: *Begin at the Parkgate Community Center at the bottom of Mount Seymour Road.*

To Get There: *If approaching from the EAST on Highway 1, take Exit 22B for Mt Seymour Parkway; if approaching from the WEST, take Exit 22. Once off the freeway, follow Mt Seymour Parkway east for 7 km to Parkgate Village Shopping Center and turn LEFT onto Mount Seymour Road. Drive 500 m and turn LEFT on Banff Court. Parkgate Community Center is on your immediate LEFT.*

Map: *Pages 148–149*

Iron Lung *Top to bottom: Senja Palonen amidst lush greenery on Hyannis Trail; stormy day over the rainforest; park sign at the base of Mount Seymour.*

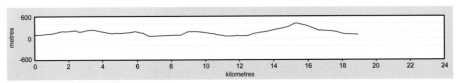

▶ Go across the power line, veer LEFT over a bridge spanning Mystery Creek and continue down to the end of the power line. Turn LEFT and descend *Mystery Creek Trail* switchbacks to *Fisherman's*.

▶ Turn RIGHT on *Fisherman's* and run to a large blue bridge (Twin Bridges) and cross over the Seymour River. Immediately turn RIGHT on *Fisherman's* and run to a well-marked junction with *Homestead*. Turn LEFT and labor up *Homestead*.

▶ At the top, turn LEFT and descend *Twin Bridges* (a gravel road) back to the Seymour River. Cross the bridge and go RIGHT along *Fisherman's* (past *Bottletop*, *Mystery Creek Trail* and *Bridle Path*) to the *Baden-Powell Trail*.

▶ Turn LEFT onto the *Baden-Powell Trail* and head uphill to Hyannis Drive. Cross the road and continue up the *Baden-Powell Trail* to the large rock step and junction with *Bridle Path* by the creek (sign). Keep RIGHT and run for 50 m to a large intersection.

▶ Turn LEFT onto the *Baden-Powell Trail*, run for about 200 m and slog up the Seymour Grind.

▶ At the obvious top-out, turn RIGHT and descend the well-marked *Severed Dick* to an intersection with *Bridle Path*.

▶ Stay LEFT along *Bridle Path* to the chain-link fence by the golf course and veer LEFT. Continue along *Bridle Path* to a junction with *Empress Bypass* (sign). Turn RIGHT and descend banked switchbacks to the *Old Buck* parking lot. Beware of speeding mountain bikes!

▶ Pass through the parking lot, pick up *Old Buck* across the road and run back to Parkgate Community Center.

■ 33 Bridle Path Circuit ♥ 8.5 km

STATS: 133 m, March–December, TH: 10 U 502006 5463368

This route is one of my favorites! The run traverses the lower slopes of Mount Seymour between *Old Buck* and Hyannis Point. It travels a good portion of the arterial *Bridle Path,* but deviates with flow along some less-traveled trails. There are a couple of notable hills, but it's mostly a rolling romp through gorgeous forest on well-established, technical trails.

The Dirt

▶ Head up *Old Buck* and stay RIGHT past the first junction with *Empress Bypass.* Contour around the road's edge before climbing to a junction with *Horse Loop* (sign). Turn LEFT on *Horse Loop* (a.k.a. *Bridle Path*).

▶ Run past an exit to *Pangor* (sign), continue along *Horse Loop/ Bridle Path,* cross over a rocky outcrop and keep going past a junction with *Empress Bypass* (sign).

▶ At a chain-link fence, veer RIGHT up *Bridle Path,* away from the golf course. Keep RIGHT past a trail leading down to Tompkins Crescent.

▶ At a junction with *Severed Dick* (a.k.a. *Good Samaritan*), turn LEFT and cross a bridge over a creek. Immediately turn RIGHT to the *C Buster* exit (sign), stay hard RIGHT and climb a steep hill (*Cardiac Hill*) for 300 m to a rocky knoll.

▶ Descend from the knoll and keep LEFT past a vague junction with *C Buster,* which is marked with an easy-to-miss cairn. Continue down a rocky hill to a major intersection with *Bridle Path* and the *Baden-Powell Trail.*

▶ Go STRAIGHT across the intersection and run 50 m to an obvious rock step (sign). Turn RIGHT, cross the creek and continue on *Bridle Path.* Keep RIGHT past *Will's Way* (sign) to reach the well-marked intersection with *Hyannis Trail* (sign).

▶ Turn LEFT and follow the wide *Hyannis Trail,* keeping LEFT past two unmarked trails. Stay on the main path to Hyannis Drive and map kiosk.

▶ Exit the trail and run the road for 100 m; turn LEFT onto the ▶▶

Access: Start at the Old Buck trailhead on Mount Seymour Road.

To Get There: If approaching from the EAST on Highway 1, take Exit 22B for Mt Seymour Parkway; if approaching from the WEST, take Exit 22. Once off the freeway, follow Mt Seymour Parkway east for 7 km to Parkgate Village Shopping Center and turn LEFT onto Mount Seymour Road. Go 1 km and turn LEFT on Anne McDonald Way. The Old Buck parking lot is on the RIGHT.

Map: Page 166–167

Bridle Path Circuit *Left to right: Weaving through beautiful, moss-covered second growth forest; a gorgeous boardwalk snakes through the terrain along Bridle Path.*

Baden-Powell Trail (sign) and follow this for several minutes. Cross a bridge and keep LEFT past two vague exit trails (to Mary Kirk Road) before reaching a junction with *Bridle Path* at an obvious rock step beside the creek (sign).

▶ At the rock step, stay RIGHT and run 50 m to an intersection. Turn RIGHT down *Bridle Path* and run 500 m to a fork marked with flagging tape.

▶ Go LEFT on *Cardiac Bypass* to the *C Buster* exit (sign). Veer RIGHT for 5 m then go LEFT across a bridge to a junction with *Severed Dick*.

▶ Turn RIGHT and continue down *Bridle Path* keeping LEFT past a trail to Tompkins Crescent (marker on tree). When you reach the chain-link fence near the golf course, stay LEFT along *Bridle Path* to a junction with *Empress Bypass* (sign).

▶ Turn RIGHT and descend banked switchbacks. (Watch for charging mountain bikes!) At the bottom of the switchbacks, cross a bridge and turn RIGHT at a junction with *Old Buck* (sign). Run 100 m back to the parking lot.

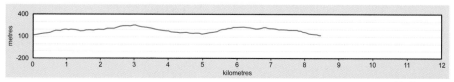

◆ 34 Dirty Diapers ♥ 7.1 km

STATS: 248 m, April–November, TH: 10 U 503145 5465051

This short stint will make you pucker… The difficulties are on *Dirty Diapers*, a very technical mountain bike trail featuring a raft of nut-shrinking wooden structures. Negotiating these is very tricky, but overall the route links plenty of fun, intermediate rainforest terrain. You'll also run past the historic Mushroom Parking Lot, an overgrown relic situated in a clearing that serves as a good gathering spot.

The Dirt

▸ From the parking area, cross Mount Seymour Road to the *Baden-Powell Trail* (sign) and run 500 m up to an intersection with *Old Buck*. Turn RIGHT and slog 800 m up *Old Buck*, crossing under the power line, to a yellow gate at Mount Seymour Road. This section is wide and rocky.

▸ Carefully cross the road and run 25 m downhill to the trailhead (sign) on the other side of the street. Enter here and head 250 m uphill to a junction (sign). Turn LEFT and run the *Old Buck Access*

▸▸

Access: Start at the Baden-Powell Trail parking lot, partway up Mount Seymour Road.

To Get There: If approaching from the EAST on Highway 1, take Exit 22B for Mt Seymour Parkway; if approaching from the WEST, take Exit 22. Once off the freeway, follow Mt Seymour Parkway east for 7 km to Parkgate Village Shopping Center and turn LEFT onto Mount Seymour Road. Drive 3 km up to a small parking lot on the RIGHT with an information kiosk and toilets.

Map: Page 166–167

Trail for 1.5 km to the Vancouver Lookout (Mount Seymour Picnic Area). Exit the picnic area and cross Mount Seymour Road. Head uphill for 100 m beside concrete barriers to a trailhead for the Mushroom Parking Lot (sign).

▶ Head 200 m downhill, past *Corkscrew,* to a junction (sign). Turn RIGHT and run 350 m to the historic Mushroom Parking Lot, which is now just an overgrown stump in a clearing. Run 5 m further and turn RIGHT (sign). Run 10 m to a fork. The left option is *Ned's Atomic Dustbin.* Instead, go RIGHT across a narrow plank system (the *Cabin Trail*) and run 250 m to reach the Mystery Creek waterfall.

▶ Continue 100 m past Mystery Creek and turn LEFT onto *Dirty Diapers* (watch for a big sign on a tree). This is the most technical part of the run. Carefully descend this terrain past creative structures to an unmarked junction with *Ned's.*

▶ Turn LEFT and run up *Ned's* for 450 m back to the Mushroom Parking Lot clearing.

▶ Keep RIGHT past signs and descend the wide *Mushroom Trail* to the power line. Continue across the power line and back into the forest. At the first junction (sign), merge with the *Baden-Powell Trail* and keep LEFT down a wide, rocky trail to a junction with *Old Buck* (sign).

▶ Keep LEFT as you run uphill for 100 m. Go RIGHT down the *Baden-Powell Trail* and descend to Mount Seymour Road and the parking area.

Dirty Diapers *Clockwise from left: An organic trail sign blends into the background; a flat stretch of trail near the Mushroom Parking Lot; brooding forest along the Old Buck Access Trail.*

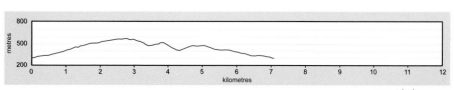

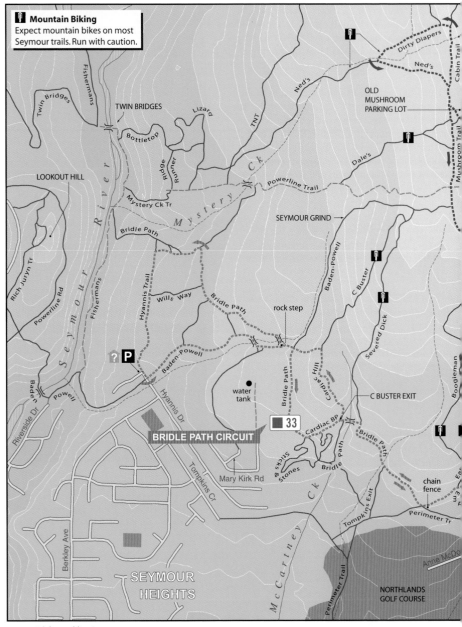

Mountain Biking
Expect mountain bikes on most Seymour trails. Run with caution.

Dirty Diapers

Ned's

Cabin Trail

Twin Bridges

Fishermans

TWIN BRIDGES

Lizard

Ned's

OLD MUSHROOM PARKING LOT

Mushroom Trail

Bottletop

TNT

Ridge Runner

Dale's

LOOKOUT HILL

Mystery Ck Tr

Mystery Ck

Powerline Trail

SEYMOUR GRIND

Seymour River

Bridle Path

Rich Juryn Tr

Powerline Rd

Fishermans

Hyannis Trail

Wills Way

Bridle Path

Baden-Powell

C Buster

rock step

Severed Dick

Boogieman

Baden Powell

? P

water tank

Bridle Path

Cardiac Hill

C BUSTER EXIT

Riverside Dr

Baden Powell

Hyannis Dr

BRIDLE PATH CIRCUIT

33

Cardiac BP

Bridle Path

Mary Kirk Rd

Sticks & Stones

Bridle Path

Bridle Path

chain fence

Perimeter Tr

Berkley Ave

Tompkins Cr.

McCartney Ck

Tompkins Exit

Anne McDo

SEYMOUR HEIGHTS

Perimeter Trail

NORTHLANDS GOLF COURSE

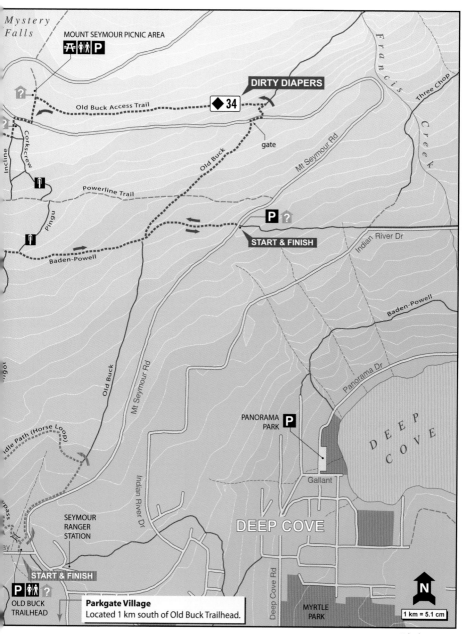

Mystery
Falls

MOUNT SEYMOUR PICNIC AREA

Old Buck Access Trail

DIRTY DIAPERS

◆ 34

gate

Corkscrew

Incline

Powerline Trail

Old Buck

Mt Seymour Rd

Francis Creek

Three Chop

Pingu

Baden-Powell

START & FINISH

Indian River Dr

Baden-Powell

Old Buck

Mt Seymour Rd

Bridle Path (Horse Loop)

Indian River Dr

PANORAMA PARK

Gallant

DEEP COVE

D E E P C O V E

SEYMOUR RANGER STATION

START & FINISH

OLD BUCK TRAILHEAD

Deep Cove Rd

MYRTLE PARK

N

1 km = 5.1 cm

Parkgate Village
Located 1 km south of Old Buck Trailhead.

◆35 Quarry Rock ♥   3.8 km

STATS: 110 m, Year-round, TH: 10 U 503671 5464127

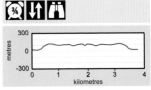

The trail to Quarry Rock follows a short stretch of the *Baden-Powell Trail* from Deep Cove to a huge cliff overlooking Indian Arm, Deep Cove and the Belcarra region (Port Moody). The view from Quarry Rock is fantastic and the trail makes for an action-packed run. It features numerous well-built bridges and is infested with roots. Several hills will torch the calories but don't worry, delectable donuts at Honey's Café will put 'em right back on!

The Dirt

▶ From Panorama Park, head north along Panorama Drive for 250 m and look for a sign for the *Baden-Powell Trail* entrance. It's on the LEFT at the foot of a private driveway.

▶ Head steeply uphill following orange markers for the *Baden-Powell Trail*. Eventually, the trail flattens out before traversing the hillside through a heavily-wooded evergreen forest.

▶ After about 20 minutes, look for a short trail leading RIGHT to an exposed bluff. If you end up at a large clearing under the power lines you've gone too far.

▶ Once you've soaked up the incredible view, retrace your steps back to Deep Cove.

Access: Start at Panorama Park in Deep Cove.

To Get There: If approaching from the EAST on Highway 1, take Exit 22B for Mt Seymour Parkway; if approaching from the WEST, take Exit 22. Once off the freeway, follow Mt Seymour Parkway east past the Parkgate Shopping Center and down a steep hill to a traffic light. Turn LEFT and follow Deep Cove Road until it banks to the right and becomes Gallant Avenue. At the four-way stop, turn LEFT on Panorama Drive and park at Panorama Park.

Map: Pages 140–141

Quarry Rock *Left to right: View of Indian Arm from Quarry Rock; amazing woodwork along the Baden-Powell Trail; Quarry Rock as seen from Panorama Park, Deep Cove.*

▲ 36 Seymour Lakes Circuit 💙💙   7.2 km

STATS: 251 m, July–October, TH: 10 U 503791 5468278

This short ramble attacks technical ground and explores the sub-alpine terrain around Mount Seymour ski resort. The first half putters around Flower and Goldie lakes (mostly in the trees) before heading back to the parking lot. The second half tackles a loop to Mystery Lake, which is far more strenuous and super choppy. It offers great views and has a nice alpine feel. Although Seymour Lakes Circuit tours a developed ski resort, the vistas, lakes, wildflowers and bears make it much more worthwhile than you might initially imagine. The trails, however, can be extra slippery when wet; I once lost a shoe in the muck!

Access: *Start at the Mount Seymour ski area parking lot.*

To Get There: *If approaching from the EAST on Highway 1, take Exit 22B for Mt Seymour Parkway; if approaching from the WEST, take Exit 22. Once off the freeway, follow Mt Seymour Parkway east for 7 km to Parkgate Village Shopping Center and turn LEFT onto Mount Seymour Road. Drive to the ski area at the top of the mountain.*

Map: *Page 173*

The Dirt

▶ Start behind the ski patrol hut at a sign for the *Perimeter Trail*. Run downhill past the Goldie Rope Tow to the Flower Lake junction (sign) and turn right. ▶▶

Seymour Lakes Circuit *Counter-clockwise from upper left: Goldie Lake reflection; Wolfang Parada cruising the Dinky Peak trail; Wolfang Parada circumnavigating Goldie Lake while Daisy shakes off a quick dip.*

▶ Quickly turn RIGHT at a second junction and run toward Flower Lake on the left. Loop around the lake before descending. Cross many boardwalks and mudholes along the way.

▶ At a four-way junction, go STRAIGHT for 25 m and turn RIGHT at the *Goldie Lake Loop* (sign). Contour around to the north side of Goldie Lake and loop back west to a junction. Turn RIGHT and run to another junction. Keep RIGHT and slog uphill to the parking area and *Perimeter Trail* signpost. It's about 3.5 km to here.

▶ From the *Perimeter Trail* sign, head west on a gravel path toward Mystery Peak chairlift base. Head uphill on *Mount Seymour Main*, which is left of the ski run.

▶ Labor up the rocky trail and turn LEFT at a junction toward Dinky Peak (sign). Keep RIGHT past a staircase to the Dinky Peak viewpoint and follow the yellow BC Parks markers over exposed rock slabs. At the bottom of the slabs, turn RIGHT.

▶ Keep RIGHT past some vague spider trails until you reach a sign where you merge LEFT onto *Mount Seymour Main*. Follow this steeply uphill to a wide ski run.

▶ Follow the ski run to a plateau, but stay LEFT when the ski run goes steeply up to the right. Quickly reach a sign, which marks the trail to the Mount Seymour backcountry, and turn RIGHT. Follow a service road around the north side of Mystery Peak to the lower Brockton Point chairlift terminal and a sign for the *Mystery Lake Trail*. With great difficulty, descend *Mystery Lake Trail* to Mystery Lake.

▶ Stay LEFT around the south side of the lake for 25 m before picking up a marked trail heading south, away from the lake. Follow this down to the base of the Mystery Peak chairlift and the parking lot.

Seymour Lakes Circuit *From top: Trailhead signpost behind the ski patrol hut; Seymour parking lot with patrol hut in foreground.*

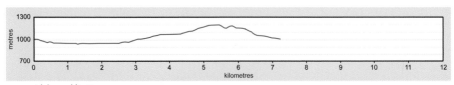

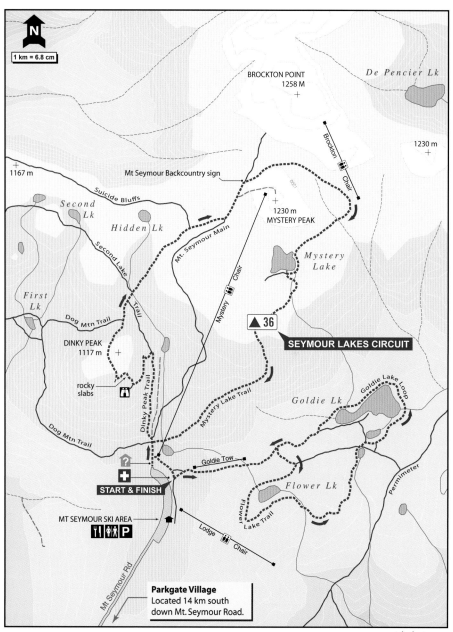

De Pencier Lk

BROCKTON POINT
1258 M

1230 m

Brockton Chair

1167 m

Mt Seymour Backcountry sign

Suicide Bluffs

Second Lk

Hidden Lk

1230 m
MYSTERY PEAK

Mystery Lake

Second Lake Trail

Mt. Seymour Main

Mystery Chair

▲ 36

SEYMOUR LAKES CIRCUIT

First Lk

Dog Mtn Trail

DINKY PEAK
1117 m

rocky slabs

Dinky Peak Trail

Mystery Lake Trail

Goldie Lake Loop

Goldie Lk

Dog Mtn Trail

Goldie Tow

Perimeter

START & FINISH

Flower Lk

MT SEYMOUR SKI AREA

Flower Lake Trail

Lodge Chair

Mt Seymour Rd

Parkgate Village
Located 14 km south
down Mt. Seymour Road.

1 km = 6.8 cm

Burnaby *Water fowl and lily pads crowd the shallows of Burnaby Lake.*

CHAPTER 3:

BURNABY

With a population of about 200,000, the satellite city of Burnaby sits immediately east of Vancouver and is bordered by the Fraser River to the south and Burrard Inlet to the north. From Vancouver, Burnaby is best accessed via Highway 1, Lougheed Highway (Route 7), or East Hastings Street/Barnet Highway. Two major park areas will be of particular interest to trail runners: Burnaby Mountain and Burnaby Lake.

BURNABY
TRAIL RUNNING ZONES

1 Burnaby Mountain Conservation Area

The prominent forested rise between Port Moody and Burnaby is the 360-metre-high Burnaby Mountain. In 1995, Simon Fraser University (SFU), which caps the mountain, donated over 800 acres of land to the surrounding Burnaby Mountain Conservation Area. The roughly 25 kilometres of trails are hugely popular with mountain bikers, runners and pedestrians, and make excellent novice to moderately difficult trail runs. Choose from several roly-poly trails that traverse the forest or get your cardio fix by climbing up the steeper trails leading to the mountaintop campus.

2 Burnaby Lake Regional Park

Burnaby Lake is the largest freshwater lake in the Lower Mainland and a popular spot for picnickers, paddlers and runners. The lake occupies a 300-hectare space immediately north of Highway 1 and south of Lougheed Highway (Route 7), in the city of Burnaby. The park features a marshy lakeshore that is home to many birds, animals,and waterfowl. The main trail encircling the lake provides a pleasant, bike-free path accessible from several trailheads.

Burnaby *Clockwise from left: Lily pads carpet the surface of Burnaby Lake; autumn maple leaf; a damp fall run on Burnaby Mountain's Mel's Trail near Simon Fraser University.*

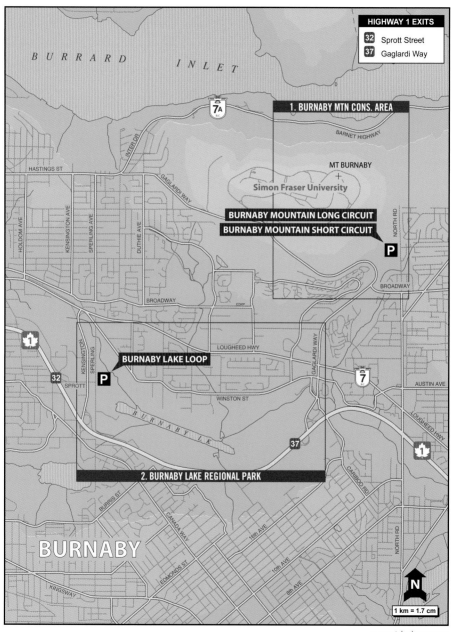

HIGHWAY 1 EXITS

32 Sprott Street
37 Gaglardi Way

BURRARD INLET

7A B.C.

1. BURNABY MTN CONS. AREA

BARNET HIGHWAY

MT BURNABY

Simon Fraser University

BURNABY MOUNTAIN LONG CIRCUIT
BURNABY MOUNTAIN SHORT CIRCUIT

P

BROADWAY

HASTINGS ST

INTER DR.

GAGLARDI WAY

KENSINGTON AVE

SPERLING AVE

DUTHIE AVE

HOLDOM AVE

NORTH RD

BROADWAY

LOUGHEED HWY

GAGLARDI WAY

BURNABY LAKE LOOP

KENSINGTON

SPERLING

P

1

32

SPROTT

7 B.C.

AUSTIN AVE

LOUGHEED HWY

WINSTON ST

BURNABY LK

37

1

2. BURNABY LAKE REGIONAL PARK

BURRIS ST

CANADA WAY

CARIBOO RD

BURNABY

EDMONDS ST

16th AVE

10th AVE

8th AVE

NORTH RD

KINGSWAY

N

1 km = 1.7 cm

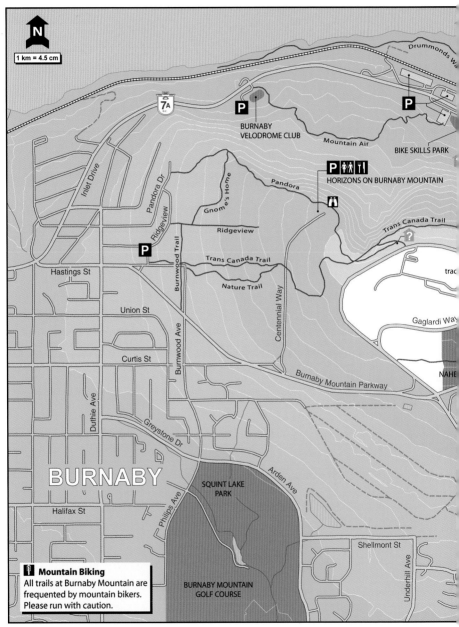

N

1 km = 4.5 cm

7A
B.C.

BURNABY
VELODROME CLUB

Mountain Air

BIKE SKILLS PARK

HORIZONS ON BURNABY MOUNTAIN

Drummonds Wa

Inlet Drive

Pandora Dr

Ridgeview

Gnome's Home

Pandora

Ridgeview

Trans Canada Trail

Trans Canada Trail

Burnwood Trail

Nature Trail

Hastings St

Union St

Curtis St

Burnwood Ave

Centennial Way

trac

Gaglardi Way

Burnaby Mountain Parkway

NAHE

Duthie Ave

Greystone Dr

BURNABY

Arden Ave

SQUINT LAKE
PARK

Philips Ave

Halifax St

Shellmont St

Underhill Ave

🔦 **Mountain Biking**
All trails at Burnaby Mountain are
frequented by mountain bikers.
Please run with caution.

BURNABY MOUNTAIN
GOLF COURSE

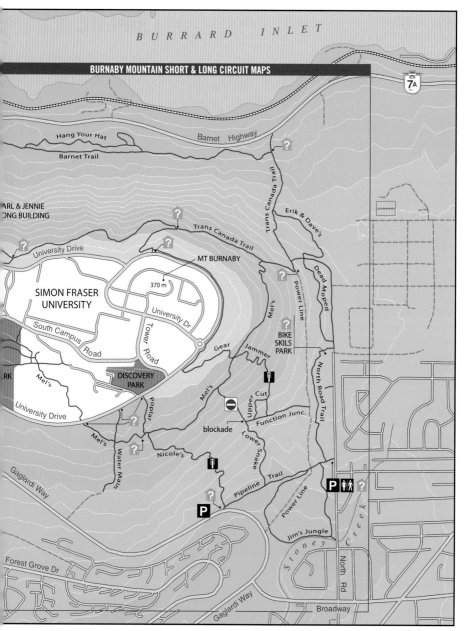

BURNABY MOUNTAIN SHORT & LONG CIRCUIT MAPS

BURRARD INLET

7A

Hang Your Hat

Barnet Highway

Barnet Trail

Trans Canada Trail

Erik & Dave's

ARL & JENNIE
ONG BUILDING

Trans Canada Trail

University Drive

MT BURNABY

SIMON FRASER
UNIVERSITY

370 m

University Dr.

Mel's

Power Line

Dead Moped

South Campus Road

Tower Road

Gear

Jammer

BIKE SKILS PARK

North Road Trail

RK

Mel's

DISCOVERY PARK

Upper Cut

University Drive

Poplar

Mel's

Function Junc.

blockade

Mel's

Nicole's

Lower Snake

Water Main

Pipeline Trail

Gaglardi Way

P

P

Power Line

Jim's Jungle

Stoney Creek

North Rd

Forest Grove Dr

Gaglardi Way

Broadway

🔲 37 Burnaby
Mountain Short Circuit ♥   6.0 km

STATS: 303 m, Year-round, TH: 10 U 507755 5457527

This fun route links *North Road Trail*, *Dead Moped*, *Gear Jammer*, *Upper Cut* and *Lower Snake* on the east side of Burnaby Mountain. Frequented by mountain bikers, this well-established singletrack sports low boardwalks and footbridges as it meanders through lush forest. One short, draining climb up the *Trans-Canada Trail* leads to an exhilarating roller coaster rip down *Gear Jammer* and *Upper Cut* that is sure to leave you with a mud-speckled, face-splitting grin.

The Dirt

▶ From the North Road parking lot and map kiosk, follow the main path for 25 m to a signed entrance for the *North Road Trail* on the RIGHT. Head into the forest and run to a gravel service road. Turn LEFT on the road and run 10 m before heading RIGHT. Continue up the *North Road Trail* to a bike skills park.

▶ Veer RIGHT through the skills park, cross a small footbridge and turn LEFT onto *Dead Moped* (moving back into the forest). Follow this to an intersection and go LEFT (uphill) to *Power Line*.

▶ At *Power Line*, turn LEFT and run 50 m to a large clearing with a map kiosk. Turn RIGHT onto the *Trans-Canada Trail* (sign) and slowly grind uphill past *Mel's* (sign), to a junction with *Cardiac Hill* (sign). Turn LEFT and slog up *Cardiac Hill* to University Drive.

▶ At University Drive, turn LEFT and follow the roadside trail for 1.5 km past a large roundabout to *Gear Jammer* (sign). Head down *Gear Jammer* to an intersection with *Mel's*. Veer RIGHT and continue down *Gear Jammer* to a signed fork with *Upper Cut*.

▶ Turn RIGHT and descend *Upper Cut* to a wide path (*Function Junction*). Veer RIGHT toward a blockade and go LEFT down *Lower Snake*. At the bottom, turn LEFT and follow the wide gravel *Pipeline Trail* (unmarked) back to the parking lot at North Road.

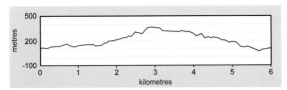

Access: The trailhead is on the west side of North Road in Burnaby.

To Get There: From Vancouver, take Highway 1 eastbound to Exit 37 for Gaglardi Way in the city of Burnaby. Head north on Gaglardi Way past Cariboo Road, Lougheed Highway, Eastlake Drive and Broadway. Continue on Gaglardi Way to the second Broadway intersection and turn RIGHT. Follow Broadway EAST then LEFT on North Road. Go about 1 km and park on the LEFT in a small gravel lot at the trailhead and map kiosk.

Map: Page 181

Burnaby Mountain Short Circuit
Late autumn running on Gear Jammer.

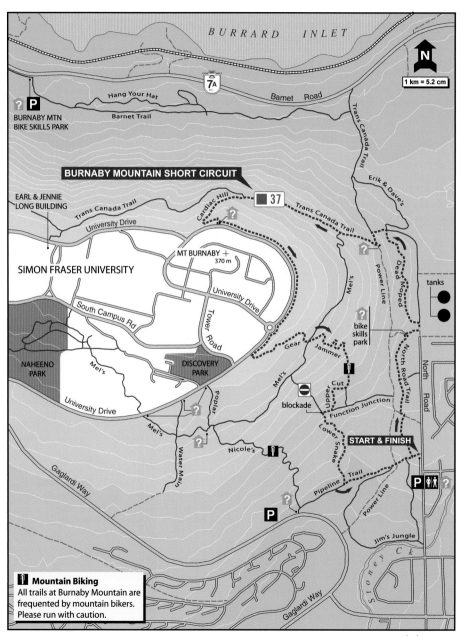

BURNABY MTN
BIKE SKILLS PARK

BURNABY MOUNTAIN SHORT CIRCUIT

37

EARL & JENNIE
LONG BUILDING

SIMON FRASER UNIVERSITY

MT BURNABY
370 m

NAHEENO
PARK

DISCOVERY
PARK

blockade

bike
skills
park

START & FINISH

tanks

🏃 Mountain Biking
All trails at Burnaby Mountain are
frequented by mountain bikers.
Please run with caution.

■ 38 Burnaby Mountain Long Circuit ❤ 9.7 km

STATS: 257 m, Year-round, TH: 10 U 507755 5457527

This pleasant outing starts with a flat, moderately-technical jog up *North Road Trail* and *Dead Moped*. After a long, slow plod up to Simon Fraser University, a short urban assault through the campus leads to a wicked descent through the mysterious Naheeno Park and a long sweet cruise down *Mel's*.

Access: *The trailhead is just off North Road, same as for Burnaby Mountain Short Circuit on page 180.*

Map: *Page 185*

The Dirt

▶ From the North Road parking lot and map kiosk, follow the main path for 25 m to a signed entrance for *North Road Trail* on the RIGHT. Head into the forest and run to a gravel service road. Turn LEFT on the road and run 10 m before heading RIGHT. Continue up *North Road Trail* to a bike skills park.

▶ Veer RIGHT through the skills park, cross a small footbridge and turn LEFT onto *Dead Moped* (moving back into the forest). Run to an intersection and continue STRAIGHT across to an unmarked trail. Continue down this twisty path to a T-junction with the *Trans-Canada Trail*. Go LEFT and climb steeply uphill to *Power Line*.

▶ Turn LEFT on *Power Line* and run 150 m to a large clearing and map kiosk. Turn RIGHT onto the *Trans-Canada Trail* (sign) and begin a draining hill climb for 800 m, passing *Mel's* (sign) along the way, to a junction with *Cardiac Hill* (sign).

Burnaby Mountain Long Circuit
Typical trail sign (below) and Senja Palonen on the popular Mel's Trail (right) in early season conditions.

▶ Keep RIGHT and follow the *Trans-Canada Trail* for 1.3 km before turning LEFT at a junction. Follow this trail to the SFU campus, where the Earl and Jennie Long Building should appear directly in front of you.

▶ Turn LEFT and run 100 m down the road before heading RIGHT on Gaglardi Way. Run past the bus stop and go underneath a concrete walkway. Continue down the left side of Gaglardi Way, past a sports field, to large T-intersection and turn LEFT. This is now South Campus Road.

▶ Run 100 m to the South Science Building and cross the street to an obvious unmarked trail entrance (for Naheeno Park). From here, pay close attention since the next several junctions are unmarked!

▶ Run down the trail for 100 m to a fork with a large stump in

the middle. Go RIGHT and follow the main path, which will likely have mountain bike tracks on it. This trail will trend right before curving to the LEFT and crossing a bridge. Shortly, another obvious bridge will appear along with a trail junction.

▸ Continue STRAIGHT across the bridge, immediately turn RIGHT and run downhill. Reach a power line, veer LEFT for 10 m and head RIGHT and downhill to University Drive.

▸ Carefully cross the busy University Road to *Mel's* (map kiosk) on the south side. Head down *Mel's* and across the *Water Main Trail* (a wide gravel path). Continue past a map kiosk, creek crossing and brief uphill switchback to a junction with *Poplar* (sign).

▸ Continue along *Mel's* for about 1 km, passing *Nicole's* (sign) and *Upper Snake* (closed). Climb a short hill and go across the power line. Check out the old VW Beetle rusting in the trees to your right.

▸ Follow *Mel's* all the way to the *Trans-Canada Trail*, passing *Gear Jammer* along the way.

▸ At the *Trans-Canada Trail*, turn RIGHT and descend to a large clearing under *Power Line* (map kiosk). Turn LEFT and run 100 m before going RIGHT down *Dead Moped* (sign) for 75 m. Turn RIGHT and retrace *Dead Moped* to the bike skills park.

▸ Continue on *North Road Trail*, veering LEFT at the gravel road intersection to return to the parking lot.

Burnaby Mountain Long Circuit *Top to bottom: The bike skills area on North Road Trail; signage for the modern Trans-Canada Trail (formerly known as Joe's Trail); forest along Trans-Canada Trail.*

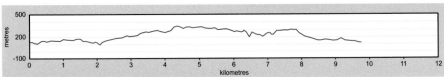

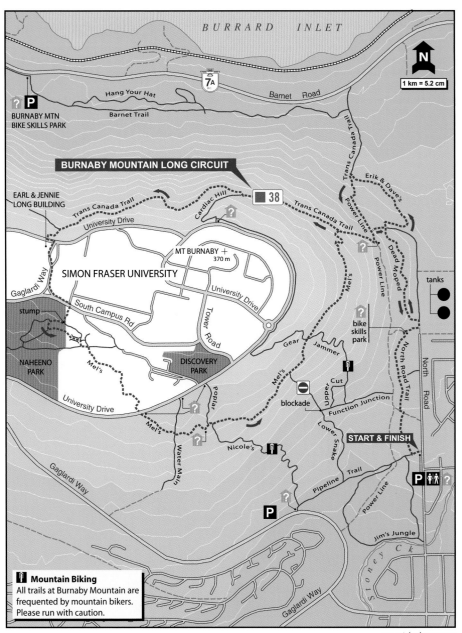

N

1 km = 5.2 cm

BURRARD INLET

Hang Your Hat

Barnet Road

Barnet Trail

P
BURNABY MTN
BIKE SKILLS PARK

Trans Canada Trail

Erik & Dave's

BURNABY MOUNTAIN LONG CIRCUIT

EARL & JENNIE
LONG BUILDING

Trans Canada Trail

University Drive

Cardiac Hill

38

Trans Canada Trail

Power Line

Dead Moped

Power Line

tanks

MT BURNABY
370 m

SIMON FRASER UNIVERSITY

Gaglardi Way

South Campus Rd

stump

University Drive

Tower Road

Mel's

Mel's

bike
skills
park

North Road Trail

North Road

NAHEENO
PARK

Mel's

DISCOVERY
PARK

Poplar

Gear

Jammer

Mel's

Upper Cut

University Drive

Mel's

blockade

Function Junction

Water Main

Nicole's

Lower Snake

START & FINISH

P

Gaglardi Way

Pipeline Trail

Power Line

P

Jim's Jungle

Stoney Ck

Gaglardi Way

Mountain Biking
All trails at Burnaby Mountain are
frequented by mountain bikers.
Please run with caution.

39 Burnaby Lake Loop   10.7 km

STATS: 133 m, Year-round, TH: 10 U 502956 5455240

One could almost pilot a Ferrari along this flat, buffed path! Considering Burnaby Lake Loop's proximity to train tracks, residential areas and nearby highways, it provides a fine natural setting and peaceful reprieve from the surrounding concrete jungle. There's not an obstacle or hill in sight, shy of dodging the geese. Nonetheless, it's a pleasant place to stretch your legs.

The Dirt

▶ From the front of the clubhouse, head south along the right-hand side of the field and turn LEFT at its end. Run 100 m before turning RIGHT at a sign, which is the start of the loop.

▶ Run a short distance, keep RIGHT at a sign for *Pavilion* and jog about 300 m to a parking lot at the Rowing Pavilion. Stay RIGHT through the parking lot and continue along the trail.   ▶▶

Access: Begin at the Burnaby Lake Sports Complex.

To Get There: Burnaby Lake sits between Highway 1 and the Lougheed Highway (Route 7) in the city of Burnaby. From Highway 1, take Exit 32 for Sprott Street. At the lights, turn LEFT on Sprott and go 1 km past Kensington Avenue to Sperling Avenue. The Burnaby Lake Sports Complex (clubhouse and fields) is directly ahead.

Map: Pages 188–189

▶ At a fork, stay LEFT before crossing a bridge over Deer Lake Brook. Stay on *Southshore*, crossing some nice boardwalks and platforms along the way, to a junction with *Avalon* after about 3.5 km.

▶ Turn LEFT and run *Avalon* past the Burnaby Equestrian Centre to some yellow barriers and a parking lot on your left. Go LEFT at the parking lot and continue on the trail to the Cariboo Dam, which crosses the Brunette River.

▶ Once across the dam, turn LEFT onto *Headwaters*. Follow this path, keeping to the left at several trail junctions, eventually reaching a large intersection and information kiosk at the Piper Spit.

▶ Continue STRAIGHT along the path, following a sign for Vancouver and *Cottonwood*, past Phillips Point viewing platform, with train tracks and freight cars on the right. After 2.6 km, the trail makes a sharp left across a bridge (Still Creek) to an information kiosk.

▶ Turn LEFT on *Pavilion* and run along the edge of the field to the parking area where you began.

Burnaby Lake Loop *Clockwise from left: Rich Wheater charges along the boardwalk at the Piper Spit; Burnaby Lake waterfowl; fall leaves line the Cottonwood Trail.*

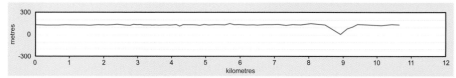

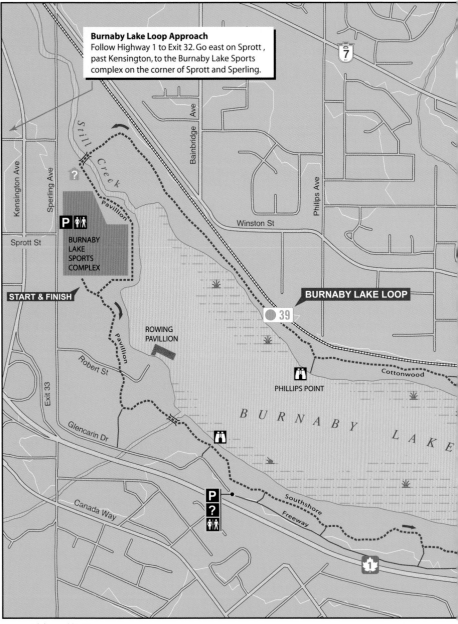

Burnaby Lake Loop Approach
Follow Highway 1 to Exit 32. Go east on Sprott , past Kensington, to the Burnaby Lake Sports complex on the corner of Sprott and Sperling.

7

Still Creek

Bainbridge Ave

Philips Ave

Kensington Ave

Sperling Ave

Winston St

P 🚻
BURNABY
LAKE
SPORTS
COMPLEX

Sprott St

Pavillion

START & FINISH

BURNABY LAKE LOOP

● 39

Pavillion

ROWING
PAVILLION

Robert St

Cottonwood

PHILLIPS POINT

Exit 33

Glencarin Dr

B U R N A B Y   L A K E

P
?
🚻

Canada Way

Southshore

Freeway

1

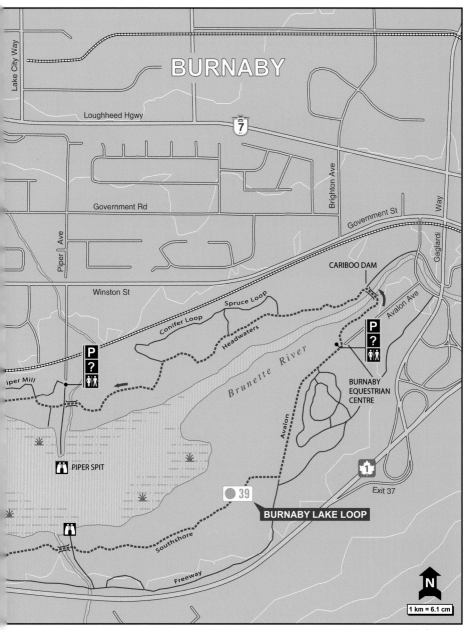

BURNABY

Lake City Way

Loughheed Hgwy

7

Government Rd

Brighton Ave

Government St

Gaglardi Way

Piper Ave

CARIBOO DAM

Winston St

Spruce Loop

Conifer Loop

Headwaters

Avalon Ave

P ?

Piper Mill

P ?

BURNABY EQUESTRIAN CENTRE

Brunette River

PIPER SPIT

Avalon

1

Exit 37

39

BURNABY LAKE LOOP

Southshore

Freeway

N

1 km = 6.1 cm

Port Moody *Buntzen Lake as seen from the Energy trail.*

CHAPTER 4:

PORT MOODY

Nestled in the eastern nook of Burrard Inlet and surrounded by mountains and ocean is the flourishing city of Port Moody. Originally inhabited by the Coast Salish nation, the "City of the Arts" is home to a creative, active community that thrives in the outdoors. Barely 30 minutes from downtown Vancouver, Port Moody rests in a spectacular setting and acts as a gateway to the rugged, emerald forests of Belcarra Regional Park and Buntzen Lake Reservoir.

PORT MOODY
TRAIL RUNNING ZONES

1 Buntzen Lake Reservoir

Just north of Port Moody and east of Indian Arm is the Buntzen Lake Reservoir. Bounded by rugged mountains, the man-made lake serves as a hotbed for recreation and is a hydroelectric power source maintained by BC Hydro. There are many high-quality trails here that appeal to hikers, runners, equestrians and mountain bikers. Open year-round, the park gets exceptionally busy in summer as the lake provides wonderful swimming opportunities. The local trails are heavily forested and Buntzen Ridge affords dazzling views over Indian Arm, Burnaby, Vancouver and Deep Cove. Don't miss the delicious ice cream served at the Anmore General Store, by the park entrance.

2 Belcarra Regional Park

Belcarra Regional Park lies adjacent to and just south of Buntzen Lake Reservoir, on the eastern shore of Indian Arm. The park is an idyllic hangout for beachcombers and picnickers who revel in the coastal ambience. The center of attention is Belcarra Beach, which has a large picnic area and beachfront access with brilliant views over Indian Arm. It is also the starting point for two short but scenic trails. Jug Island Beach and Admiralty Point make nice, mellow destinations in their own right, but when combined give a fine tour of Port Moody's western waterfront.

Port Moody *Top to bottom: Indian Arm and Belcarra as seen from Quarry Rock in Deep Cove; Kristina Jenei cruises the Jug Island Beach Trail; the water-worn granite of Admiralty Point with Indian Arm in the background.*

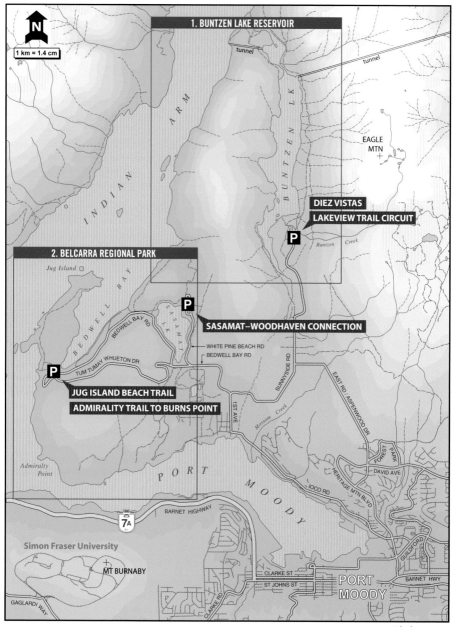

N
1 km = 1.4 cm

1. BUNTZEN LAKE RESERVOIR

tunnel

tunnel

INDIAN ARM

BUNTZEN LK

EAGLE MTN

DIEZ VISTAS
LAKEVIEW TRAIL CIRCUIT

P

Buntzen Creek

2. BELCARRA REGIONAL PARK

Jug Island

BEDWELL BAY

SASAMAT LK

P

SASAMAT–WOODHAVEN CONNECTION

BEDWELL BAY RD

WHITE PINE BEACH RD
BEDWELL BAY RD

SUNNYSIDE RD

TUM TUMAY WHUETON DR

P

JUG ISLAND BEACH TRAIL

ADMIRALITY TRAIL TO BURNS POINT

1ST AVE

Mossom Creek

EAST RD / ASPENWOOD DR

Admiralty Point

PORT MOODY

IOCO RD

HERITAGE MTN BLVD

FOREST PARK

DAVID AVE

GUILDFORD

7A
BC

BARNET HIGHWAY

BARNET HWY

Simon Fraser University

MT BURNABY

CLARKE ST
ST JOHNS ST

CLARKE RD

PORT MOODY

GAGLARDI WAY

40 **Lakeview Trail Circuit**   13.0 km

STATS: 199 m, March–December, TH: 10 U 510373 5465103

This is a mellow ramble along the lower slopes of Buntzen Ridge on the west side of Buntzen Lake. The trail weaves and bobs with flow, as it migrates between the power lines and some old-growth forest sections. Along the way you'll encounter several hills, but nothing that's too nasty or very long. Make your return via the well-traveled *Buntzen Lake Trail*, a wide gravel path virtually free of obstacles. It's a perfect pony ride.

Access: Start at the Buntzen Lake Reservoir parking lot in Port Moody.

To Get There: From Highway 1, take Exit 26 for East Hastings Street/Route 7A, just south of the Second Narrows Bridge. Zero your odometer and follow East Hastings Street through Burnaby for 5.2 km to where the main road splits.

Veer LEFT on Inlet Drive, which soon turns into Barnett Highway. Follow Barnett Highway into Port Moody and at 13.7 km turn LEFT on St. John's Street/Route 7A. At 16.6 km turn LEFT on Ioco Road. At 17.5 km, go STRAIGHT through the lights and up Heritage Mountain Boulevard, following signs for Buntzen Lake.

At 19.5 km, turn RIGHT at a roundabout onto David Avenue and quickly turn LEFT onto Forest Park Way. Make another LEFT on East Road (Aspenwood Drive) and, at 23 km, turn RIGHT on Sunnyside Road. After 24 km, arrive at Buntzen Lake Reservoir and follow the road into the parking area. (Park hours: 8:00 a.m.–6:00 p.m.).

Map: Page 199

Lakeview Trail Circuit *Clockwise from left: Finishing up along Buntzen Lake Trail; signs point the way; BC Hydro's Burrard Pumphouse; Buntzen Lake.*

The Dirt

▸ From the information kiosk in the main parking area at Buntzen Lake, head to the southwest corner of the parking lot and the start of the *Buntzen Lake Trail* (sign). Follow this flat gravel trail south, passing *Energy* on the right. Keep right past two more trails, both of which lead back to the road.

▸ Reach a floating bridge and cross an interesting swamp. At an intersection with Pumphouse Road, turn RIGHT and run 1.25 km to the pumphouse and information kiosk. Turn LEFT onto *Lakeview*.

▸ Run *Lakeview* for 250 m to an intersection with *Saddle Ridge*. Continue STRAIGHT through on *Lakeview*.

▸ Cruise along *Lakeview* for 4.25 km. Along the way, you'll come within inches of your return route as the trails come very close to each other in a couple of spots. *Lakeview* dodges in and out of the power lines as it meanders along moderate singletrack. Numerous steep, tight and loose descents will test your braking skills! At the north end of the trail, continue past a detour to a viewpoint and drop down to the power lines and a trail junction.

▸ Turn RIGHT on the *Old Buntzen Lake Trail* and go 100 m to another sign for *Buntzen Lake Trail* and South Beach, which is near the lakeshore.

▸ Turn RIGHT and head back on the *Buntzen Lake Trail*, passing several swampy bays filled with logjams. This leads to the pump house and information kiosk.

▸ Run Pumphouse Road back to the floating bridge. Cross the bridge, keep LEFT and retrace your steps back to the parking area.

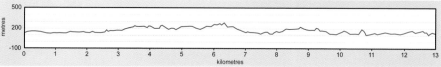

▲41 Diez Vistas Trail ♥♥♥ 13.2 km

STATS: 457 m, May–November, TH: 10 U 510373 5465103

Diez Vistas is one of the best adventure runs in this guide as it offers an outstanding challenge in technical running, route finding, hill climbing and descending. Initially, the route leads steeply up and over Buntzen Ridge and has fabulous views over Indian Arm. This section is strenuous, remote and laden with obstacles. The return route along the *Buntzen Lake Trail* is very different. It follows a heavily-travelled, packed-gravel path that winds through an amazing forest of old-growth trees that literally drip with moss. This stretch gives way to the clean, inviting waters of the nearby lake.

Access: *Start at the Buntzen Lake Reservoir parking area, same as for Lakeview Trail Circuit on page 194.*

Map: *Page 199*

The Dirt

▶ From the information kiosk in the main parking area at Buntzen Lake, head to the southwest corner of the parking lot and the start of the *Buntzen Lake Trail* (sign). Follow this flat gravel trail south, passing *Energy* on your right. Keep right past two more trails, both of which lead back to the road.

▶ Reach a floating bridge, cross it and go STRAIGHT across Pumphouse Road to *Diez Vistas* (sign). Head up *Diez Vistas* for 10 m and turn RIGHT at a sign for *Horseshoe* and *Diez Vistas*. Follow orange markers uphill for 1.5 km to junction with *Sasamat* and continue STRAIGHT to the power line. The trail continues across the power line, a little up and to the left (yellow markers).

▶▶

Diez Vistas Trail *From left to right: February cruising along Buntzen Ridge (both); Brent Nixon near the Punta del Estes variation.*

▶ Struggle up steep switchbacks for 850 m to a junction where a variation (*Punta del Este*) goes to the right. Keep LEFT here and almost immediately you'll pass a good viewpoint on the left. Continue up the trail and keep LEFT at the next junction (going right will lead back to the *Punta del Estes* viewpoint).

▶ Reach the top of Buntzen Ridge and run through open forest past all ten viewpoints. (Vistas 1 and 2 are the best and feature rocky outcrops with stunning views down to Deep Cove, North Burnaby and the mouth of Indian Arm. Beware of abrupt cliffs at Vistas 5 and 6!) At Vista 10, descend rock slabs and re-enter the forest.

▶ Continue down the burly trail to an old skid road and turn RIGHT. After about 100 m, go LEFT at an unmarked junction. Head down a rough trail to the Powerhouse Road.

▶ Turn RIGHT and run under power lines to a sign for the *Old Buntzen Lake Trail* (straight ahead is an old water intake station). Turn RIGHT and run under the power lines. Keep LEFT past a junction with *Lakeview* to a sign for North Beach. Turn LEFT and run 250 m to a suspension bridge. Cross the bridge and trend RIGHT across North Beach. Here you will find picnic tables, toilets and good swimming.

▶ Run past the Port Moody Tunnel information kiosk and DANGER sign before veering LEFT up a short trail to Powerhouse Road.

▶ Turn RIGHT and run for 5 m. Turn RIGHT again on *Buntzen Lake Trail*. Follow this well-built track, past several left-hand exits to Powerhouse Road, toward South Beach and the parking lot. There are numerous bridges along the way and the lush forest drapes dramatically over the trail, perfect for a heroic sprint to the finish.

▶ As you approach South Beach, go LEFT at the dog area fence. At the next junction, turn RIGHT and cross a bridge before veering left toward the parking lot.

Diez Vistas Trail *Grinding up the switchbacks to Buntzen Ridge (top) and Spanish signage along the ridge*

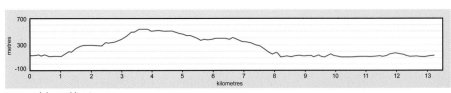

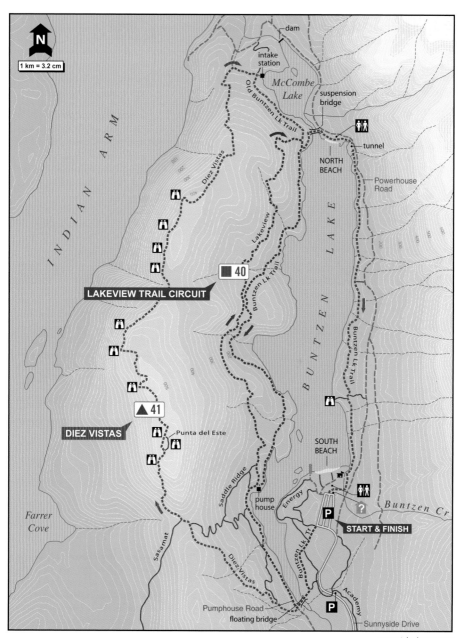

N

1 km = 3.2 cm

dam

intake
station

McCombe
Lake

suspension
bridge

Old Buntzen Lk Trail

I N D I A N   A R M

Diez Vistas

tunnel

NORTH
BEACH

Powerhouse
Road

Lakeview

40

LAKEVIEW TRAIL CIRCUIT

Buntzen Lk Trail

B U N T Z E N   L A K E

Buntzen Lk Trail

▲ 41

DIEZ VISTAS

Punta del Este

SOUTH
BEACH

Saddle Ridge

pump
house

Energy

Buntzen Cr

P

?

Farrer
Cove

START & FINISH

Sasamat

Diez Vistas

P

Pumphouse Road

floating bridge

Academy

Sunnyside Drive

www.richwheater.com

STATS: 178 m, Year-round, TH: 10 U 508286 5463436

This cruise offers straightforward running around scenic Sasamat Lake before tackling a rougher, hillier side trip to Woodhaven Swamp. If you don't feel up to the running this entire circuit, simply jog around the glimmering lake. This cuts the distance and difficulties in half, plus you get to cross a cool floating bridge. Note that White Pine Beach is off-limits to dogs, but there is a signed paw-path that detours around the beach allowing passage for Fido.

Access: Start at the White Pine Beach parking area on Sasamat Lake in Belcarra Regional Park.

To Get There: From Highway 1, take Exit 26 for East Hastings Street/Route 7A, just south of the Second Narrow Bridge. Zero your odometer and follow East Hastings for 5.2 km to where the main road splits. Veer LEFT on Inlet Drive, which soon becomes Barnet Highway. At 13.7 km, turn left on St. John's Street/Route 7A and drive through Port Moody.

At 16.6 km, turn LEFT onto Ioco Road. At 17.5 km, go LEFT at the lights and continue westbound on Ioco Road. At 21.3 km, turn RIGHT on 1st Avenue and veer LEFT onto Bedwell Bay Road. Follow signs for Sasamat Lake, turn RIGHT onto White Pine Beach Road to find the parking area.

Map: Page 205

Sasamat–Woodhaven Connection
Clockwise from left: The clean, fresh waters of Sasamat Lake; a stand of dead timber at Woodhaven Swamp; no dogs allowed at White Pine Beach; boardwalk around Woodhaven Swamp.

The Dirt

▶ From the parking area at White Pine Beach, head toward the lake following "paw" markers for the dog path detour near the right (north) end of White Pine Beach. This leads to a yellow gate and wide path just above the concession stand. Turn LEFT and start running.

▶ After 200 m, turn LEFT (sign) and drop down to the lakeshore. Turn RIGHT and follow a bomber trail along the lake. After 450 m, climb a short staircase to a gravel road and turn LEFT. Run past cabins to the Sasamat Outdoor Center entrance. Cross the road, cross Windermere Creek and run to a junction (sign).

▶ Turn RIGHT toward *Woodhaven Swamp Loop* and run beside a concrete wall leading to Bedwell Bay Road.

▶ Cross the road and head up the trail for about 1.5 km to an unmarked junction with a service road. Turn LEFT toward a paved road, ignoring the unmarked *Springboard Trail* on your left.

▶ Cross the road (Tum-tumay-whueton Drive) and continue along the obvious trail ahead (*Springboard*). After 200 m, turn LEFT at an interpretive sign. Run 10 m down the trail and turn RIGHT onto the unmarked *Woodhaven Swamp Loop*. Run around the swamp for 1.25 km and return to the same junction. Turn RIGHT and run uphill for 10 m before turning RIGHT back onto *Springboard*.

▶ Cross the road again, pass *Springboard* and turn RIGHT at the second trail entrance. Follow the path back down to Bedwell Bay Road.

▶ Cross the road to the trail and turn RIGHT. Keep RIGHT and follow *Sasamat Lake Loop* for 900 m to a floating concrete bridge. Cross the bridge and turn LEFT.

▶ Duck under an interesting tree as you charge along the lakeshore. As you approach White Pine Beach, go RIGHT and follow the dog detour back to the parking lot above the beach.

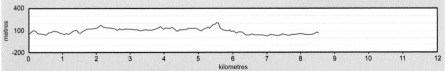

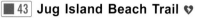

43 Jug Island Beach Trail ♥   5.1 km

STATS: 79 m, Year-round, TH: 10 U 505466 5462235

Leading from the Belcarra Beach picnic area is a sweet little trail that ushers you to a quaint barnacle-studded beach overlooking the coastal oasis of Jug Island. Much of the trail is packed gravel snaking through rainforest, but there are some short, steep sections and just enough rough stuff to keep things interesting.

The Dirt

▶ From the Belcarra Beach parking area, head past picnic gazebos to the trailhead signpost. Run a short distance, cross the road and turn LEFT following signs for *Jug Island Beach Trail*. From here it's hard to go wrong.

▶ After 2.5 km, a short descent deposits you at a small beach with the compact Jug Island straight in front of you. When you're done skipping stones, turn around and head back along the same path.

Access: The trail starts at Belcarra Beach parking and picnic area.

To Get There: Follow the Sasamat–Woodhaven Connection directions (page 200) to the turnoff for Sasamat Lake/White Pine Beach. Continue along Bedwell Bay Road and turn LEFT at the next fork onto Tum-tumay-whueton Drive. Follow this to Belcarra Beach parking and picnic area.

Map: Page 205

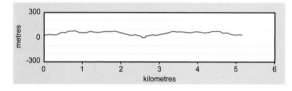

Jug Island Beach Trail *Kristina Jenei in shadows on Jug Island Beach (below) and on the Jug Island Beach Trail (right).*

44 Admiralty Trail to Burns Point 5.3 km

STATS: 42 m, Year-round, TH: 10 U 505466 5462235

This run is slightly longer but much flatter than the *Jug Island Beach Trail* and offers good running flow with great views of the inlet. It leads from Belcarra Beach past Admiralty Point to Burns Point and provides several waterfront access points along the way.

The Dirt

▶ From the Belcarra Beach parking area, head past the toilets toward the beach and locate the *Admiralty Point Trail* sign by a kayak tour shack. Run the trail to a private gravel road, turn LEFT along the road and watch carefully for a sign where the trail leaves the road. Be careful not to accidentally head left up to *Springboard* or wander too far right toward some private residences.

▶ Cruise along the *Admiralty Point Trail* past awesome viewpoints at Cod Rock and Admiralty Point, eventually reaching Burns Point after about 3 km. Turn around and head back the way you came.

Access: *The trail starts at Belcarra Beach parking and picnic area, same as for Jug Island Beach Trail on page 202.*

Map: *Page 205*

Variation: If you want to tackle a hearty 12 km circuit, run from Belcarra Beach to Jug Island and back, then run the *Admiralty Point Trail* to Burns Point and back.

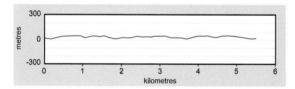

Admiralty Trail to Burns Point *Kristina Jenei running through fall leaves on Admiralty Trail (left) and traversing an outcrop of seaside granite at Admiralty Point (right).*

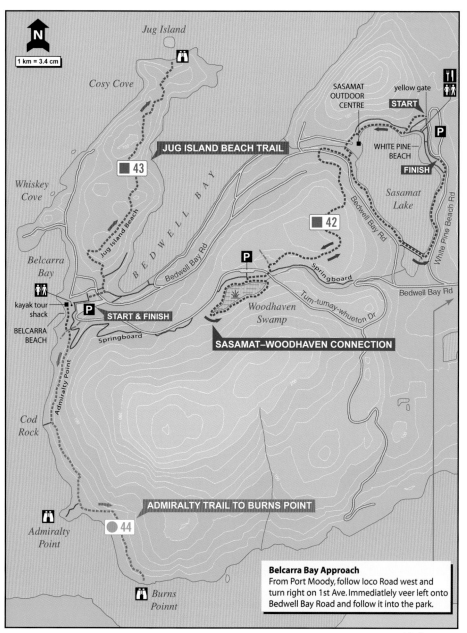

N

1 km = 3.4 cm

Jug Island

Cosy Cove

SASAMAT OUTDOOR CENTRE

yellow gate

START

JUG ISLAND BEACH TRAIL

WHITE PINE BEACH

FINISH

Sasamat Lake

Whiskey Cove

43

BEDWELL BAY

42

Bedwell Bay Rd

White Pine Beach Rd

Jug Island Beach

Belcarra Bay

Springboard

P

kayak tour shack

Bedwell Bay Rd

Woodhaven Swamp

Tum-tumay-whueton Dr

Bedwell Bay Rd

START & FINISH

BELCARRA BEACH

Springboard

SASAMAT–WOODHAVEN CONNECTION

Admiralty Point

Cod Rock

200

ADMIRALTY TRAIL TO BURNS POINT

44

Admiralty Point

Burns Poinnt

Belcarra Bay Approach
From Port Moody, follow loco Road west and turn right on 1st Ave. Immediatley veer left onto Bedwell Bay Road and follow it into the park.

EMERGENCY & MUNICIPAL CONTACTS

Organizations

www.clubfatass.com

www.mountainmadness.ca

www.fitnessvancouver.ca

www.nsmba.ca

www.bmba.ca

Events

www.5peaks.com

www.runthenorthshore.com

www.kneeknacker.com

www.dirtyduo.com

www.ironlung.ca

www.mudrunride.com

www.adventurechallenge.ca

www.diezvista50.ca

www.theyeti.ca

DIAL 911 FOR ALL EMERGENCIES

North Shore Rescue (NSR)
www.northshorerescue.com
147 East 14th Street
North Vancouver, BC
(604) 983-7441

North Vancouver RCMP (police)
www.rcmp.ca/bc/lmd/nvan/index/htm
147 East 14th Street
North Vancouver, BC
(604) 985-1311

West Vancouver Police
www.wvpd.ca
1330 Marine Drive
West Vancouver, BC
(604) 925-7300

Lions Gate Hospital
www.lghfoundation.com
231 East 15th Street
North Vancouver, BC
(604) 984-5813

Vancouver Police
www.city.vancouver.bc.ca/police
2120 Cambie Street
Vancouver, BC
(604) 717-3321

Metro Vancouver Parks
www.metrovancouver.org
4330 Kingsway
Burnaby, BC
(604) 432-6200

Busters Towing
www.busterstowing.com
(604) 685-8181

Drake Towing
www.draketowing.com
(604) 251-3344

Vancouver General Hospital
www.vch.ca
2775 Heather Street
Vancouver, BC
(604) 875-4111

St. Pauls Hospital
www.providencehealthcare.org
1081 Burrard Street
Vancouver, BC
(604) 682-2344

UBC Hospital (Koerner Pavilion)
www.vch.ca
2211 Westbrook Mall
(604) 822-7121

Burnaby General Hospital
www.bhfoundation.ca
3935 Kincaid Street
Burnaby, BC
(604) 434-4211

Coquitlam Search & Rescue
www.coquitlam-sar.bc.ca
Town Centre Fire Hall
1300 Pinetree Way
Coquitlam, BC
(604) 927-3484

Eagle Ridge Hospital (Port Moody)
www.erhf.ca
475 Guilford Way
Port Moody, BC
(604) 461-2022

NOTES

NOTES

NOTES